COURAGE
& FAITH

Spiritual Guidance for Overcoming Adversity,
Finding Meaning, and Living a Purpose-Filled Life of Success

Johnny Griffin

COURAGE & FAITH

Spiritual Guidance for Overcoming Adversity
and Living a Purpose-Filled Life of Success and Meaning

Johnny Griffin

PUBLISHED BY: JOHNNY GRIFFIN
ISBN: 978-0692133132

For further info, please contact the author at: hilltopsoldier@gmail.com.

DEDICATION

This book is dedicated in honor of my mother, Eula Gines. She taught me love through application, as well as a determination to live life as God had purposed! Because of her commitment, faith, and sacrifice, she served as a role model that allowed me to persevere in writing this book. May you rest in peace.

To my lovely wife, Melissa Griffin (aka Lisa), daughter Jezell, and son Jevontez; you are truly what matters most in my life.

To my host of siblings: Willie Ann, Cornelius, Isiah, Londale, Eugene, Bettie, Ulysses (aka Bo), Margaret, Otis, and Ulisa; I love you all dearly.

To anyone who has the desire to excel despite unwanted challenges and circumstances that you have or will experience in life, this is your opportunity to discover everything that you are seeking and deserve.

And finally, I would like to dedicate this book to the Sunday school teachers and men's ministries across the world, who all do inspiring and important work in God's name.

TABLE OF CONTENTS

CHAPTER 7

It's Never Too Late . . . Start Now!.....p59

CHAPTER 8

Your Heart Holds the Key to Your Purpose.....p69

STUDY GUIDES

ACKNOWLEDGMENTS

Thanks be to God for giving me the vision of fulfilling my dream of making this book a reality.

I would like to thank my publishing company, Let's Write Books, Inc. and their editor for their professional advice and assistance in writing and publishing this book.

A special thanks to my one and only mentor, Randy Brotherton, who helped me on my career path. Thank you for taking an interest in my career growth and development, and for giving me my first job opportunity in the federal government. You were always there to provide me with sound advice and encouragement.

And thanks to those trailblazers who inspired me and give all of us a glimpse into their lives through books, conferences, and plays: Bishop T.D. Jakes, Joel Osteen, Oprah, and Tyler Perry.

INTRODUCTION

Blessed is the one who perseveres under trial because,
having stood the test, that person will receive the crown
of life that the Lord has promised to those who love him.

~ JAMES 1:12 (NIV)

Since you've picked up this book, I am going to assume that you are facing challenges in life, or that someone you know is. Maybe you're living through a difficult period, and you're not sure how to get through the tough times. Or maybe you have been living with obstacles your entire life, and wonder how things could ever possibly change for the better.

Do you ever feel you're not getting what you want? Do you sometimes feel that life is unfair? Do you believe that you never get any breaks? If you can relate in any way to what I'm saying, then this book is for you.

I know, because I once felt the same way.

However, I've also learned that no matter how bad things may be, it is possible to turn things around. No matter how bleak the situation, and no matter how hopeless you may feel at the moment, this book is going to serve as your roadmap toward living a life of meaning.

I have learned and finally know in my heart that it *is* possible to make something out of my life – even when the challenges seemed too great. I know now that I *can* succeed, even though there were so many times in the past that I couldn't even begin to fathom how that could ever happen.

You need to know the same thing: you *can* make something out of your life – even if you can't see a way at this moment in time. You *can* get past your challenges. You *can* succeed. And you *do* have something very important to offer the world. God has created you and has given you a special set of talents and gifts. You just need to unlock that power that already exists within you.

Now, before you argue that there's no way you could possibly have something important to contribute, realize that discovering those gifts and unleashing the greatness within yourself is not always easy. I've learned that lesson the hard way.

Throughout my life, I've become somewhat of an "expert" when it comes to facing obstacles. Growing up in the rural town of Santuck, two miles from the city limits of Marvell, I lived a relatively happy life, yet there were many times when I got the sense I wasn't as privileged or have the same opportunities that other kids around me had. I was one of eleven children to a single mom whose husband died at an early age, and we struggled to make ends meet. Many of the struggles I recall were financial, as it would have been difficult for a single mother in rural Arkansas to provide for her eleven children.

Fortunately, my mother was a selfless individual who continually made sacrifices to provide for our basic needs. But when it came to other areas in life, there were things I missed out on that the other kids seemed to take for granted. These became major obstacles for me. For example, each year my classmates would return from summer vacation, talking about hunting, fishing, or camping trips they took with their dad. I could never boast about taking one of those trips. My mother did her best, but she couldn't provide those kinds of luxuries – and without a father figure in my life, those experiences were impossibly out of reach. When I got older and moved out of Arkansas, I enlisted in the military and got to know quite a few kids who had trust funds. *Trust funds?* What *are they?* I would ask myself.

I had to learn to grow up be a man – and a father – without having that all-important male role model in my life. Yes, I had brothers who were older, but they were preoccupied with their own lives and challenges. I would observe them and learn what to do (and not do), but nothing could truly take the place of having a father.

As I got older, other obstacles became apparent to me. I had a strong desire to become better educated, but I didn't know how. Without a trust fund or the financial means to attend college, I didn't appear to have many options. The military or factory work were the typical paths an impoverished kid in my area would follow, so I chose the military. While I would learn later that the military could provide me with the educational access I desired, I didn't know that at the time. Instead, I thought attending college right out of high school was the only way to receive that all-important education.

Speaking of education, leads me to some other experiences that are indelibly etched in my memory – and that contributed to my belief that I just couldn't get any breaks. While I was a good student at school, I certainly didn't have some of the opportunities others in my town had. When I say "opportunities," I'm talking about some of the privileges, or the chance to forge certain relationships with teachers, that accompanied being part of a prominent family. Sadly, these opportunities did not have anything to do with how much one studied, hard work, or intelligence.

While it wasn't fair, there were definitely kids in town who would receive better grades and scores simply because of their family's social standing. For example, my brother once told the story of being out late the night before a test with one of his football buddies, and neither took the time to study. Panicked about the test that they did not prepare for, they traded answers while they took the exam in class. Both boys turned in papers with identical answers. The only difference? Their backgrounds, as my brother's friend came from a prominent, well-to-do home. When the students got their tests returned, guess who got the good grade – and guess who did not. It did not matter that their answers were the same. My brother got the poor grade. As for his buddy with the influential family? He got an A.

This imbalance and inequity surfaced through relationships with the teachers, too. In today's news, we hear about teacher-student scandals, but these kinds of relationships were happening in my hometown long before they became the fodder for CNN, NBC, and Fox. I distinctly remember how one of my teammates from football got involved with the coach's wife. It started when she said, "I hope you boys win today," and then proceeded to wager a bet that if we won, my buddy had to go on a date with her!

We won the game, the two went on a date – and they kept on dating. Once the coach caught wind of this, he and his wife got divorced. But the relationship continued between my teammate and the coach's ex-wife, and the two eventually married.

Perhaps even more interesting is that this same classmate lived on a street where several other students were dating teachers at the school, too! Of the kids on that street alone, three or four were dating staff members at my school. It wasn't uncommon for any of them to visit with their girlfriend (the teacher) at night, and she would ask them to help grade our tests. Or, if there were an upcoming quiz or test, the teacher would let the student look at the test and answer key the night before. Of course, there was a lot of favoritism – and little fairness.

With the deck stacked against me, it would have been easy to fall back on excuses. None of those situations were fair or ethical, but that was my reality. These were the obstacles I faced. While the kids who were at the top of the class were offered free rides to college, I had earned my grades honestly – but without a family that could help me make dreams of college a reality. In fact, as you'll learn later in this book, one of my family members actually did everything in his power to prevent me from ever going to college, even when there was a glimmer of hope that I could attend!

Those were just a few of the challenges I faced in life, and each one affected my well-being profoundly. Growing up with a single mom meant I never had a role model to know how to become a true man and good father. I carry that pain with me even to this day that I never had a dad alongside me, teaching me.

Meanwhile, some of the injustices at school began to sour me on the unfairness of it all. Fortunately, I learned how to turn those roadblocks into learning experiences. And when I was presented with role models and positive examples, I seized on those people and moments to better myself.

You can do the same.

In this book, I will share anecdotes from my life, and the lives of others, to illustrate that no matter what obstacle you face, there are right and wrong ways to approach it. I'll teach you the lessons that I've learned the hard way, in the hope that you can learn from my mistakes, model my successes, and ultimately find a successful path toward living a life of meaning and purpose.

There are two ways you may choose to interact with this book: The first way is to simply read the book from start to finish. You'll see there are "Worth the Discussion" segments in each chapter. These exercises will ask you to consider an idea or think about your answer to a thought-provoking question. You can use "Worth the Discussion" as a prayer point to meditate on throughout the day as you absorb the ideas and concepts and integrate into your life the success strategies presented in that chapter. This is a powerful way to make a difference in your life if you are working through the book on your own.

Another way to proceed through this book effectively is with the support of a study group. I've provided study questions at the back of the book, with separate study guides for adults and teens. Simply work with a trusted group as you read this book; after each chapter, flip to your specific group's set of questions, and work together toward answering and discussing the questions and topics. For instance, if you are part of a men's Bible study group, you may choose to read chapter 1 before you meet. During your meeting, discuss the "Worth the Discussion" prompts in that chapter, and then work through the chapter one questions that begin on page 80.

Now that I've shared a little bit about my life, please take a few moments to reflect on your own life. What obstacles are you facing? What feels like an insurmountable challenge in your life? What events – both positive and negative – have led you to where you are today? What are your hopes for your life? What do you wish to achieve after reading this book? Finally, are you going to work through the exercises in this book on your own – or are you going to work on them with a trusted group of friends, family members, youth group, Bible study group, etc.?

Whatever your dreams are, and wherever you are on your path to living a meaningful life, you can start moving forward NOW. I look forward to sharing the journey with you!

COURAGE & FAITH

CHAPTER 1

What is Real Success?

*Take delight in the Lord,
and He will give you the desires of your heart.*

PSALM 37:4 (NIV)

It wasn't until I was an adult that I realized how much my mother provided for us. She was always making sure we had what we needed, despite the sacrifices she had to make. I was always observing, watching and studying her. She wanted the best for her children but didn't always have the means to provide it. While she always took care of our basic needs – food, clothing shelter – I didn't realize how much we were missing at the time. To me, it was a good life…

But then I began to compare myself to other people – and everyone seemed to be ahead of me, in every respect.

When I joined the Army in 1988, I remember feeling different from those around me. For the first time, I was surrounded by a very large group of diverse people. Having to go through the various trainings, I heard about other people's experiences, and I began to believe that they were intellectually superior to me when I compared what they said with my educational background. They seemed to be in a better position in life, and that intimidated me. It caused a lot of self-doubt.

Up until that point, I hadn't realized how much of a gap existed, and meeting all these new people made me realize how sheltered my life had been. That's when I knew that my education might not have prepared me for the college education I desired. Not only that, but I became exposed to people with more material wealth than I had ever seen. I looked around and thought I saw success everywhere: big houses, nice cars, trust funds, and well-educated people. How could I catch up? How could I compete, so to speak?

In the face of these realizations, I had a choice: either give up or continue to work. As a determined person, I decided to put in the work, and I learned through my failures and others' failures – as well as learning from others' successes – and all of it helped me grow. It also helped me develop a strong moral compass and the understanding of what success is – and what it isn't.

Discovering What True Success Is – And Isn't

Before you can embrace true success in your life, it is important to realize that there are false definitions of success in society. Look around at anyone you deem successful and realize that your perception of that person's success may be false, misleading or downright dangerous to buy into. For example, there were some people around me during my early adulthood whom I had considered to be "successful." These were the people who always seemed to be "ahead" of me – and my belief about their success came from the way they presented themselves to others, including me.

They were great speakers, and if you would simply listen to their words, you just wanted to buy into what they said. Their ability to speak well helped them to become very influential; but as I got to know some of them better, I discovered the truth: there was little substance behind their words. Sure, they would sound good and try to stroke your ego as they told you how you should be living your life – but then I found that what they were telling me wasn't even working for them!

Before I realized that these smooth talkers were not always who or what they appeared to be on the surface, I would become frustrated. Why couldn't I speak like them? Why wasn't I on the fast track in the same way? Why didn't I have it all together? Luckily, I figured out that their words were just that – something that sounded good to my ears but was not grounded in results – and was not proven to work, seeing that it didn't even work for the person talking. Really, their "success" was a façade.

On the other hand, there are people I have met who have truly become successful in their lives, but it is easy to be fooled into thinking their success happened instantly and effortlessly for them. I don't believe in "overnight successes." The people you see who have "made it" by certain standards have sacrificed and put in the work behind the scenes that you know nothing about. The good news is that you, too, can succeed – but understand that to get to the same point may require consistent sacrifice from you, and work behind the scenes for a long time.

Another important point is to be mindful of who your role

models are. As I mentioned, some of the people who I thought had "arrived" were really just slick talkers who didn't have substance to back up their words – while other people truly succeeded after getting honest with themselves and putting in the work to improve their lives and overcome their obstacles.

The easiest way to differentiate between those who are truly successful and those who pretend to be successful is to dig deeper. Get to know that person, and find out what helped him or her get to the spot where he or she is today. Learn more about their lives, relationships, and lifestyle. What you find may help you in your own life – or it may reveal that they aren't as "together" as you thought.

I learned this lesson after envying the big houses people I knew lived in, along with the nice cars they drove. Growing up in a three-bedroom house was tight for eleven children and our mom. By age 17 or 18, I would drive around and dream about how nice it would be to live in the palatial homes I would pass. Eventually, I was able to get inside some of those homes, and, to my surprise, several of them had no furniture inside! The parents had stretched themselves so thin to purchase the beautiful house that looked impressive and rich from the outside, that they had nothing left to put inside the home. Suddenly, I wasn't quite so envious, knowing that they made the trade-off of being stretched thin financially to make their outward appearances look a certain way. I was able to apply this to my life by knowing that I didn't want to live a life of financial stress.

For me, success means having peace of mind – knowing that I can provide for my family. Yes, I like nice things – homes, cars, and clothes. But I have discovered the art of indulging in the finer things in life without inflating my lifestyle to a point that I can't afford it.

What you see on the outside of my home is what you see on the inside – and the same can be said for me as a person. What you see on the outside reflects the person I am inside as well.

The way I show up in the world is an honest demonstration of my core beliefs and values. I won't try to sell you on a lifestyle or moral code that I don't live or believe in myself. I've never been a chess player, but I'm always thinking ahead to decide on my next move in life. Looking ahead has allowed me to anticipate possible problems and avoid them, or learn how to navigate around them successfully.

Focusing on Other People's Success Will Distract You from Yours

Webster's Dictionary's definition of success is "the accomplishment of an aim or purpose." There is nothing like living decades yet never arriving at the place in life that you so desire. If your success is to accomplish what your neighbor has accomplished, then you might be working to achieve a success that was not meant for you. The sad part of achieving this kind of success is that, while you may succeed in the same way your neighbor has, perhaps that kind of success was intended for his or her life, but not yours. So, for you, it may not be a true success, and you may never be satisfied – despite the accomplishment.

Society gives us false perceptions of what success really is. And people play into this myth by attempting to look successful, even if they know that they are living a lie. If you really listen to people and get to know them, you will find that many are no further along in life than you are. Many have mastered the art of pretending to be that which they really are not. Others strive to live a certain lifestyle and pretend to be someone they are not, leading others further from their own purpose.

If you look at others' successes as examples for building your own success, then you will be free to pursue the success that you were uniquely created for. This will allow you to become the person you are destined to be, and at that point you will understand the meaning of true success. When success is viewed and understood from the right perspective – a Godly perspective – one is in a better position to achieve success for the life that was intended for him or her.

Godly Success

The most important success in life is Godly Success: success that will move you toward your intended destiny, because it ultimately impacts the lives of others. Godly Success means living a life that serves others in a way that was uniquely created for you. When you measure your success by your ability to impact and influence the lives of those around you and future generations, then you will realize success beyond your wildest dreams.

Even if you must experience many setbacks and challenges along the way, it will be worth it in the end. It is all too easy to become selfish, looking for any markers of success that only benefit you. I'm sure that if God only focused on selfish "success," we would not exist.

True success hinges on serving humanity. That will provide you with the best life possible, and you will experience more success in life than you ever thought you could achieve. There is nothing wrong with observing what you may consider a success in others, but their success was not meant for you and will never be the measure of your success. Instead, when you view and understand success from the right perspective, you are in a better position to achieve success for the life that was intended for you.

I am led to pray a simple but powerful prayer as Jesus prayed for us. Father, forgive us, for we know not what we do. Your life doesn't belong to you. My life does not belong to me. It belongs to God.

When you put your life in God's hands, He can guide you to the success your heart desires.

Getting Honest

In addition to understanding that another person's success is not your success, honesty is the key to living a truly successful life. The honesty that Jesus exhibited in his life serves as a prime example to all of us regarding the importance of truthfulness, even when it is difficult to do.

When young Jesus disappeared after his family's annual Passover pilgrimage to Jerusalem, his parents were worried. When they finally found him, they realized he had remained in the temple, asking the elders questions and astonishing them with his wisdom. Mary approached Jesus and asked, "Son, why have you done this to us? Your father and I have been frantic, searching for you everywhere." (Luke 2:48, NLV)

Jesus replied, "But why did you need to search? Didn't you know that I must be in my Father's house?" (Luke 2:49, NLV)

They did not understand the statement that He had made to

them, since they did not understand that He was the true Son of God. In today's society, Jesus's answer to his mother could easily be perceived as disrespectful, and it also could have been an uncomfortable moment for Jesus to speak in such a way to his mother. It would have been easy enough for Jesus to fabricate a story to explain his whereabouts, but He decided to tell the truth to Mary – even if she didn't completely understand the implications of His words. Like Jesus, you need to have a Luke 2:49 mentality and be willing to be honest, even in difficult circumstances.

The actions and words of Jesus clearly illustrate the importance of honesty. Honesty assures others that we can be trusted, even in difficult circumstances. Honesty ensures that we will receive everything God has planned for our lives. Without a doubt, honesty will allow you to find your way past, through, and around life's hurdles so you can become a true, Godly success.

Being honest means admitting your personal shortcomings and mistakes instead of succumbing to a victim mentality. When I thought everyone was so far ahead of me in life, I had to admit who and where I actually was: I was a kid who did not receive the best education in high school, and I grew up somewhat sheltered. I wasn't privy to some of the experiences that other kids my age had, and I would never know what it was like to grow up with a father in my life.

After this honest assessment of my life and myself, I stopped looking to other people for comparison purposes. After that honest appraisal, I could face my obstacles head-on. For example, if I wanted that A+ job, I had to ask myself, "Johnny, do you have A+ knowledge or experience?"

If the real answer was no, then I had to admit it – and then proceed to put in the work to qualify myself for what I wanted. While others may blame external factors when they don't get what they want in life, I found that acknowledging my shortcomings and then working to improve them allowed me to stop feeling victimized. I was empowered to take control of my life. Of course, certain things are out of my control, yet there is more within my grasp to change than I had ever imagined. The more I seized every opportunity to get honest with myself, the less those uncontrollable outside factors made a difference in my life.

Growing up in the church reinforced the importance of being obedient and bringing God into my life by keeping Him at the center. Living my life in this way, I have been able to become 100% honest with myself, and I finally seeing it paying off. Living the way the God wants me to live has allowed me to reap rewards. Being obedient has given me many blessings and victories.

Once I finally admitted I didn't have the best educational background, that admission allowed me to finally move forward, attend college, and earn a degree. Being honest allowed me to recognize my financial limits, and while I have been able to provide nice homes and cars for my family, I've never allowed myself to overspend to try to impress others. This has given me financial peace of mind, without the stress that so many people feel who have over-leveraged themselves. These are just some of the changes I noticed once I got honest with myself.

Time to Get Honest with Yourself

Now it's time for you to get honest with yourself. To do this, you need to face the adversity in your life and embrace it. Yes, embrace your crisis! That's because during these difficult times you have the greatest opportunity to learn and to grow. If life is too easy, you'll forget about your struggles. You'll become complacent, and you won't be motivated to change.

Instead of trying to ignore your challenges or wish them away, ask yourself questions in the midst of the struggle. For instance, if an opportunity exists at work, but you don't receive that raise or promotion, ask yourself some hard questions. Could you actually do that job? Do you have the skills and experience? Or do you first need to learn and grow? Ask yourself these tough questions, not in order to put yourself down, but to assess your strengths and weaknesses, so you can begin to work on the areas where you need to improve your skills, knowledge base, or interactions with others. Be honest – and then make sure you're in a position to be qualified for the next opportunity.

Learn along the way through your trials and experiences, and by all means be transparent. One of the greatest problems I see is that we're not willing to tell the stories of our downfalls, struggles and shortcomings. Maybe you want to succeed, but you look at those around you and start getting depressed. Realize that those around you may have gone the struggles you are going through at an earlier period in their lives. In my case, I was consistent in working on myself, and people who are struggling today might not realize at first that I went through the very same experience they are going through – but I worked through that dark time and have made it to the other side.

Some of the members of our men's group may be a bit envious because they didn't do what they should've done in life and feel they aren't in the same station in life where they see me. But they're not really willing to talk about it, and if they just had discussed honestly how they're feeling, they would understand that they are in good company. And the people who have "arrived" probably had to work through their obstacles to get there. Every one of us can get there, but not without effort!

So the next time you are struggling, be honest enough to talk to others around you about it. You may find there are more people than you think who have worked through the very same obstacle! And even if they haven't had an identical experience, I am confident that there is probably some roadblock that they have needed to work through in their lives. If they can share with you how they survived their difficult time, it may help you apply some of their principles and strategies to your life as well.

I don't believe that people wake up in the morning and go out into the world with the intention to make mistakes, do bad things, or fail. I think they just don't know any better. And sometimes, as they get older, they simply don't know how to change. It's okay if you aren't at the place you think you "should" be in life; you may be embarrassed, but it's more important to admit what you don't know, because from that point you can focus on areas for improvement, learn from others, and change.

Steve Harvey is an example of someone who is very transparent. He speaks about how he went to college, but started to fail. He had to admit to himself that college just wasn't for him. He realized that being transparent is important, and it allowed him to move on with his life in a positive direction.

I talked for years about rental properties, but I realized that for years I had been doing just that – only talking. Reading about Steve Harvey's life inspired me, and I got honest with myself by admitting that talking about it would never make anything happen. I finally decided to invest in real estate and generate some passive income for myself – and it worked! We love to look at "where they're at now," when it comes to successful people, but we usually don't know how they got there. Most of them had to put in the work. By getting honest, seeking help, and working on yourself, you too can become the success that God wants you to be.

Worth Discussion

Challenging situations and circumstances are bound to happen, but you must learn to endure. It is easy to give up when faced with difficulties in life, but, as the saying goes, "If success were easy, everyone would be able to do it." It's also easy to compare yourself to others and decide that you're falling short.

The key is, don't quit; if you quit, you will never know your purpose for being created. If God had felt like quitting, He wouldn't have provided His awesome examples for enduring. You were created for more than just existing in life. You were created to make an impact in the lives of others and serve as an example to encourage others and lift them up when life becomes challenging. Perhaps most importantly, you must be willing to be honest with yourself, even in difficult circumstances.

Ask yourself: Where am I in life today, and what do I honestly need to change to get where I want to go?

CHAPTER 2

The Importance of You

A conviction that you are [a child] of God gives you a feeling
of comfort in your self-worth. It means that you can find
strength in the balm of Christ. It will help you meet the
heartaches and challenges with faith and serenity.

~ JAMES E. FAUST

In Chapter 1, you discovered that society's definition of success is
fleeting and hollow, while Godly success will fill your life with a sense
of purpose and meaning. At the same time, in order to live the life
God meant you to live, you must first honor the importance of who
you are and what you have to offer the world. Although this may
seem paradoxical at first (How can I focus on myself while being
selfless?), it really does make sense upon closer inspection: you must
first appreciate your own value before it is possible to become a true
servant to others and experience a measure of success that transcends
society's narrow definition.

Sadly, many people – including me, in the past! – cling to myriad insecurities and fears that have the potential to prevent them from appreciating their own value. This limits their ability to reach their full potential and to make a profound difference in the world.

When I was preparing to retire from my position in the military, I was not sure what I wanted to do with my life – though I knew I wanted to do something meaningful. In the midst of grappling with this, I attended a graduation event where people were receiving their doctorates. One of the speakers told the group, "Don't allow your degree to just hang on a wall." He even went one step further and recommended that everyone go out and write a book. Boy, did that strike a chord with me!

For years, I had harbored a fantasy of being a writer. Even as far back as 2007, when I was stationed in Korea, I would have dreams and ideas at night and then jot down their content when I awoke. Initially, I wasn't sure what I should do with these random writings, but I felt that those dreams and ideas that kept coming to me were important – and I felt a strong need to write them down.

Eventually, I began to wonder how it would feel to author a book. Well, I almost dismissed the thought as soon as it crossed my mind. You see, those insecurities I carried with me from not having the best educational background as a child caused me to doubt myself. Eventually I overcame those challenges and even earned my Master's Degree in Business, graduating Magna Cum Laude, I almost let those fears kill the dream before it could even take root.

As I listened to the graduation speaker that day, I felt something come alive from deep within; I began to envision myself as an author. I began to believe I really did have an important story to tell. As my confidence grew, I started doing research online and came across a publisher. I reached out to him, and even though I was excited, some of that fear would creep back in. It became a bit of a tug of war: in one moment, I would tell myself that I wasn't qualified, and in the next moment I would be convinced I had a story to tell that would help other people with their lives.

The more I talked to people, whether it was teaching Sunday school, giving a sermon, or speaking to a brotherhood, the more I realized that there were many people who could relate to what I was saying; they were connecting with me because of my words.

With time, I overcame my nagging fears and knew for certain that I needed to get my story out into the world. I remembered how Oprah encouraged Tyler Perry, telling him to write it all down. With all these thoughts in my head, I finally mustered the courage and said to myself, You know what? I'm going to do it! Why not?!

So I drove to a Starbucks, grabbed a cup of coffee, and started typing freely on my laptop. And throughout my journey to publishing these words, I have experienced an unbelievable sense of freedom and peace, knowing that I will leave a legacy to the world, just by telling my story.

What is the Story Inside of You?

Within each of us there is a story. Maybe it is buried deep inside or maybe it just waiting to get out. Either way I can assure you that it is there! And when you to start to take ownership of your unique story, you will begin to fully appreciate who you are as a person and be in a position to share your special contribution with the world.

CHAPTER 2

Know that whatever your story is, it will most likely apply to other people's lives. There are certain eternal truths, and those same truths will hold true a century, two centuries, or even 300 years from now. Plus, you never know what sharing your story will lead to; maybe you'll change somebody's life, or maybe it will open up a door that had been previously unknown or closed to you. Or maybe telling your story will lead you to some place or somebody that's really interesting in one way or another, and they'll find their way to you through your words. Maybe someone halfway around the world finds your book and wants to translate it into several languages. You never know. Of course, there's no guarantee that these things will occur, but it's possible that they can – as they have for others. You never know, but if you don't share your story, those things will never even have a chance to happen.

In the movie The Words, a man had written a manuscript inspired by events from his life. He had completed the draft, but in a strange twist of events, his girlfriend left the manuscript on the train – only for someone else to discover it. The person who discovered the manuscript was an author, and he decided to submit it to a publisher as his own work. It wasn't until the original author read the book that he realized that his words had been stolen – and the accolades had been given to someone else! I still think about the anger and regret this man must have felt when he realized someone stole his story, how he should have received credit for his words and ideas – but never would. And I think of the guilt that the supposed author must have grappled with, knowing full well that the story under his name was not his to tell.

Only you can tell your story, and whether it is more formally through a book, video, pictures, a play, poetry, a song, or more simply by talking about your experiences with someone else, what you have to say does matter and can make a difference.

Finding Your Story

You may be reading this chapter, thinking, This advice is great if you want to be an author. But that is not a dream of mine. I have other dreams!

Understand that finding your story has more to do with discovering who you are as a person than aspiring to become a writer. Finding your story is all about identifying your strengths and unique qualities, where they came from, and how you developed to become the person you are right now. It may also help you understand and form your identity as you find your place in the world.

Through much self-reflection, I've learned that empathy for what others are going through is one of my strengths. Because I grew up with some hardship and struggles, I know how that feels. I know that your income level doesn't define you, and I also know that you don't need to let your past dictate your future.

Becoming more self-aware has allowed me to use my struggles to become a stronger individual – and by my sharing what I've learned with others, they know there is someone out there who understands them. In addition, I can serve as an example to others, showing that it is possible to achieve success in life despite circumstances that seem to conspire against you. By making the choice to learn from others' mistakes and follow positive role models like my mother, I have been able to find my place in the world as a unique child of God who can help others realize their self-worth.

Take the time to do the same – find your story! To fully appreciate how important you are, reflect on your life, and consider the path you have taken to get to this point. Recognize the positive and negative choices you made, and think about how those decisions have affected you. Take into account important people in your life as well. Think about how they have impacted you as a person.

Finally, celebrate the fact that these varied experiences make you incredibly unique. Realize that – imperfections and all – you are a special person. No matter where you are in your life, and no matter how close (or far) you are from your goals, the ability to know yourself positions you to discover your true purpose and create a positive roadmap toward your destiny!

Worth Discussion

Whatever it is that makes you "tick" is important to discover, because it is only then that you can share your story, gifts, and talents with the world.

Now, it's time to ask yourself: What choices have I made in life, and how have these choices affected me? Who and what has influenced me? In what ways?

When you can answer these questions, you will have a stronger sense of your personal identity, and you will be ready to take the next steps in your life – and find your true purpose.

CHAPTER 3

The Secret to Finding Your Destiny

If you're alive, there's a purpose for your life.

~ RICK WARREN

Once you begin to appreciate yourself and recognize your worth, you are ready to consider your purpose in life. If you already have a dream and goals, great! You are one step closer to making your mark in the world. But what if you don't know what you have to offer? What if your fears have tricked you into believing you don't have any talents? That you don't have anything meaningful to say or share? In that case, please take time to ask yourself, "What was I created for? What could I do to leave the world in a better place than where I found it?"

If you're finding it difficult to generate ideas, begin to discover your true purpose by talking to people who know you; preferably, people who know you well. Ask them what they consider to be your talents and gifts. What do they think you have to offer the world? What do they think you're good at? Sometimes others can see something in you that you fail to see in yourself.

Another way to think about this is to consider what you hear others complaining about. What are people negative about? Have you ever had success in solving that particular problem? If not, could you find a way to make that situation better? Perhaps you have the answer to a problem that others are grappling with. Ask yourself, How can I make society better? How can I play a positive role, instead of just complaining about it?

Finally, do your best to avoid tunnel vision as you keep in mind the big picture. When you watch a television show, you might not notice everything on the screen because you are too busy focusing on the dialogue between the two characters, the chase between the police officer and the criminal, etc. People do the same thing in life: they only focus on one aspect of their lives, not noticing everything else that is going on around them. If you can be on the lookout for people, circumstances, and opportunities that are already around you but that you may never have taken notice of before, you are in a better position to move toward your purpose – or discover what your true purpose is during your time in this world. Who knows? You may have a dream – and the means to achieve that dream are right there in front of you, but you never noticed before!

There's No One Like You

Your purpose is unique, because there is no one else in the world who is exactly like you. Maybe you are a talented woodworker. You may realize your purpose in life by putting your talents to use building beautiful furniture. Because you allow your true gifts to shine through, others can appreciate and benefit from your ability to express yourself – and enjoy what you have to offer!

Perhaps you're a mom who others turn to for advice. Rather than diminishing your role in the world by making self-deprecating statements like "I'm just a mom," or "I don't have a real job," take pride in what you do! Raising children is the most difficult occupation out there. To successfully raise kids – and notice that I said successfully, not perfectly! – is no small feat. If others seek you out for your words of wisdom, they do this for a reason. It's because you have a gift in this area. And rather than ignore your gift or minimize it, celebrate it and allow it to serve others.

Remember that your purpose is not going to be the same as your neighbor's. And your purpose doesn't need to lead to fame or fortune, either. Sometimes people only think they are successful if they're the next LeBron James or Michael Phelps. You don't need to be a high-profile athlete, politician, actor or actress to leave your mark.

Also, we already have an Oprah Winfrey in this world. We already have a Will Smith. We don't need a clone of someone who already exists. We need you. We need somebody who is ready to create his or her own life – instead of trying to live someone else's. It's not so much about looking outside yourself as it is about looking inside yourself and acknowledging what unique contribution you are making or could make to the world.

I'm Johnny, and the world needs a Johnny. The same goes for you. The world needs you – and the unique gifts you bring into this world.

Unlocking Your Destiny with Honesty

Being honest with yourself will allow you to truly recognize your strengths as well as your weaknesses. As you discover your true purpose, you must remain honest with yourself, and being honest may require you to step outside of yourself so you can see yourself. It may require that you get out of your comfort zone.

If you rationalize and tell yourself lies, you will keep yourself stuck in your comfort zone and never realize your purpose. For instance, if you tell yourself you're qualified to be the next CEO of your company – but you're actually lacking some skills and are really not ready for this advancement – you'll simply make excuses as to why you didn't get the promotion. You'll rationalize that your company isn't fair, and that you can never get any breaks.

Instead of being completely honest and then working on yourself to build the skill-set to match the job you desire as you pursue a dream, staying in your comfort zone means that you remain in your current job, complaining to your colleagues about how unfair life is. Believe me, there will be plenty of people who want to commiserate with you! That's because they, too, don't want to be honest with themselves. They don't want to admit they might be able to change their circumstances – because that would mean they need to have some faith and step out into the unknown.

Breaking Free From Your Comfort Zone

To break out of your comfort zone requires changing some of your thought patterns. If you think about something enough – even when you don't always feel it or totally believe it – you most likely will begin believing it, knowing that you can succeed at it.

For instance, if you know that it's important for you to hone your public speaking skills to realize your dream – but you're not even comfortable speaking in front of a small group – then you may need to join a toastmasters group to practice. As you begin to speak in front of others, you'll feel petrified. But with new and improved thought patterns, you can start telling yourself, I can do this! I can speak in front of these people – and they want to hear what I have to say!

Of course, at first you may feel that you're "lying" to yourself, but what you're really doing is establishing the reality that you wish to bring into your life. You have already been honest with yourself in admitting that your skills are weak. Now you are reinforcing the better version of yourself that you intend to manifest.

With time and practice, you'll wake up one day and realize, "Hey! I really am an effective public speaker! I've come a long way, and people really do enjoy listening to what I have to say."

If you are serious about growth, whether it be personal, professional, or spiritual growth, you must be willing to embrace risk, do away with fear, and make changes in your life.

Any time you step out of your comfort zone requires taking a risk and exposing yourself to new possibilities. However, you will feel so much better when you work the vision that you seek for your life. I have met many people who simply want their vision – yet they don't work that vision. The Bible is clear: "You shall eat the good of the land" (Isaiah 1:19, ESV). However, you need to work the land in order to "eat the good" of it, and sometimes that work will involve going past your discomfort. It is important that you understand this concept so you can receive the best for your life, for this will not only give you the results you seek but will also keep you focused, no matter how many challenges you encounter.

You need to be able to move forward, even when you aren't certain what will happen, how it will happen, or when it will happen. You won't even know for sure how you'll respond if that which you've been hoping and praying for arrives! However, the more you act "as if" and tell yourself the story you want to see in your life, the more you will prepare yourself for your dreams manifesting. It is important to know that it is always better to be prepared; then, when the moment presents you with an opportunity, you can seize it.

Get By With a Little Help From...God

True living requires faith and confidence in God. Life deals us way too many unknowns for us to be able to predict everything that will happen during our lifetimes. We are not the creators of the world and mankind, but that doesn't mean we need to live hopeless, helpless existences. Rather than backing away from challenges – or becoming paralyzed by fear – know that there is someone way more powerful than any human being that can help...and that is God.

So many people miss out on life's opportunities because they let fear hold them back, or they try to live someone else's life. Whatever God has planned for you, it is custom-made for you, and you alone! His plan is not for your cousins, nephews, sisters, or brothers. Never has this been more clear than when we contemplate our fingerprints. God has made each set exquisitely unique – a true symbol of how special each and every one of us is in God's eyes!

So when the time comes to discover our true destiny, and we get scared, we don't need to fear the unknown! Lean on God, and He will give you the strength, faith, and resolve to remain determined and persevere, no matter how many obstacles may be in the way.

Think about people like Dr. Martin Luther King, Nelson Mandela, and Oprah Winfrey. Or consider the trailblazers in the television ministry that we have the privilege of knowing, like Joel Osteen and TD Jakes. While your destiny may not look the same as theirs, realize that each one of them needed to step out of their comfort zone and put in the work to get to where God was leading them.

It amazes me that so many people dream of being prosperous and successful, yet never do anything to achieve it. I guarantee if you talk to anyone who has experienced success in life and asked him or her if it was necessary to step out of his or her comfort zone and have faith, that person will, without a doubt, say yes!

I also suspect that these successful people had to stop trying to measure themselves against others. Playing the comparison game is tiring, and it's a game you'll never win. There will always be someone who is prettier, more handsome, smarter, wealthier, or more spiritual than you. If you get caught up in these comparisons, you will eventually tire of not being able to "win" and you may even decide to quit!

The only standard you need to measure up to is God's standard, and His standard never changes. He does not expect you to be identical to anyone else. He simply asks you to appreciate what you have been given and use it to serve others.

Where to Find Joy

The feeling of joy doesn't come from status, salary, sex, or success. Joy comes from acts of service. God designed you to be joyous when you give yourself for the sake of others – mainly because He wants you to be as He has created you to be. It is all about giving love as He gave of His love. John 3:16 tells us: "For God so loved the world that He gave His only begotten Son." Only those who give of themselves for His sake will ever experience what it means to have a fulfilling life. Giving your life requires sacrifice and commitment, and you must make it a part of your everyday living in the application of service and generosity, just as your Creator did.

As Matthew 20:28 says: "Even the son of man came not to be served but to serve others and to give His life as a ransom for many" (NLT). What I remember about my mom is that she always had a capacity for giving to others, even though her bucket of material and monetary resources was usually low or almost empty. Her selflessness in helping others was an important lesson for me, as it taught me what it means to give from the heart.

Giving from the heart requires you to get in that place where God would have you be. Sometimes that place will be way out of your comfort zone. When looked at the right way, discomfort could be your best option for your current situation and even for your future. Being uncomfortable at times can help you to stay on the path or journey that you need to be on, in order to achieve your goals and serve others. It all comes down to you.

No matter what you do, remember to keep God in your life. This is the best way to discover your true purpose, because God will lead you if you heed His call. He will direct your steps, nudging you toward a life of meaning that is fulfilling to you while being life-giving and life-changing to others.

How I Got Started

When determining my purpose, I began by assessing my life. I asked myself: Where am I? Where do I want to be? How can I play a part to make an impact on others? That's how I started making changes in my life and seeing them through.

There were times in the past when I needed to assemble a team so we could collaborate and work together toward a common cause. I knew part of my purpose was to motivate others to follow my leadership and influence them, but how could I get them to buy in? Through self-assessment and awareness, I realized I needed to listen more and accept different viewpoints, acknowledging that my way of doing things wasn't the only way to complete the project. I had to recognize that there might be a better way. It's a great lesson to learn: when you learn how to embrace change, you will grow into a better version of yourself.

When Kodak closed its doors, part of the problem for this company was that they didn't adapt and change with the times. Instead of pivoting and adjusting to the new demands and opportunities that accompanied the digital era, the camera giant remained bound to their original business model, reveling in past success with cameras and film. Eventually, they couldn't compete anymore, and they became obsolete, going bankrupt in just a few years.

I realized that, in my life, if I approached situations with that Kodak mindset – thinking I could rest on my laurels – then I, too, would be phased out by new, better ideas and ways of operating. I did not want to become obsolete, so I learned to open my mind and continue to learn and to grow.

Reading inspirational books and meditating on their messages was extremely helpful in expanding my horizons as well. People like Joel Osteen and Bishop TD Jakes have inspired countless people through their words and advice, and these are just a few of the people I turned to as models of inspiration.

I also turned my attention away from unwelcome situations and circumstances and instead turned toward the promises that God had waiting for me. I remembered the words in Jeremiah 29:11 (NIV): "'For I know the plans I have for you,' declares the Lord, 'plans to prosper you and not to harm you, plans to give you hope and a future.'"

There are other Scriptures that gave me encouragement at the right time, too. For example, when I became overly concerned about challenges I encountered, I needed to stop allowing myself to get discouraged and just keep moving on. Even if I felt I had taken 1,000 steps already, I only needed to take one more step in order to walk into the blessings I had been seeking. Psalm 37:23 (KJV) reinforced this notion of remaining focused and patient: "The steps of a good man are ordered by the Lord: and he delighteth in his way." Faith in God and the words in the Bible take courage, but knowing that God is always with me gives me the strength I need. God was with the children of Israel and others in the Bible, even in trying times, and I know that God will provide me with the same fortification he gave them when I need it the most.

Finally, when it comes to finding your purpose, remember that, no matter what your dream is, it all begins with a thought. Before the Wright brothers took flight, there was a thought. Before Einstein made amazing discoveries, there was a thought. Before I wrote this book, there some initial ideas and thoughts. Once you have that thought, if you simply factor in some faith, confidence, and courage, you will find that it becomes possible to realize your vision and live a better life.

Worth Discussion

Isaiah 43:3 states: "When you pass through the waters, I will be with you; and when you pass through the rivers, they will not sweep over you. When you walk through the fire, you will not be burned; the flames will not set you ablaze." This message reminds us that God will see us through anything; however, we must remember that stepping out into unfamiliar terrain may bring with it some discomfort as well.

Joel Osteen says, "I want to challenge you today to get out of your comfort zone. You have so much incredible potential on the inside. God has put gifts and talents in you that you probably don't know anything about."

Now ask yourself, "What comfort zone do I need to escape to live a life of courage that will allow me to step out on faith, realize my full potential, and serve the world?"

CHAPTER 4

Trust the Journey

Faith is your anchor and sustainer in the new season. Faith helps you see in the dark. And when you feel like you can't see, faith steadies your heart to trust that you know what is true."

~ T.D. JAKES

Shortly before dawn Jesus went out to them, walking on the lake. When the disciples saw him walking on the lake, they were terrified. "It's a ghost," they said, and cried out in fear.

But Jesus immediately said to them: "Take courage! It is I. Don't be afraid."

"Lord, if it's you," Peter replied, "tell me to come to you on the water."

"Come," he said.

Then Peter got down out of the boat, walked on the water and came toward Jesus. But when he saw the wind, he was afraid and, beginning to sink, cried out, "Lord, save me!"

Immediately Jesus reached out his hand and caught him. "You of little faith," he said, "why did you doubt?"

And when they climbed into the boat, the wind died down. Then those who were in the boat worshiped him, saying, "Truly you are the Son of God." (Matthew 14: 25-33, NIV)

In your life, there are going to be times when you cannot guarantee the outcome from your actions and choices. You may be faced with a difficult decision, and the best choice is not clear to you. Or, you may face a decision in which you know what the right choice is, but it is not going to be easy.

Whenever you are faced with these difficult circumstances and decisions, it is imperative that you put your trust in the journey – and the best way to do that is through trust in God.

Notice that in the story of Peter and Jesus, Peter is willing to trust Jesus when the water is calm. Clearly, the Son of God is allowing him to walk on the water without sinking, and Peter is experiencing this supernatural ability. However, as soon as the wind kicks up and the conditions on the water begin to deteriorate, Peter loses faith and panics. As a result, he begins to sink until Jesus grabs his arm to steady him.

Sometimes we are like Peter: willing to trust God when times are good, basking in the blessings He provides for us. But what about when things don't go well? What happens when we receive a terrifying medical diagnosis? Or one of our children gets involved with the wrong crowd? Or we lose a job? Or a family member suddenly passes away? These are the storms in our lives that will test our faith and resolve, because the outcome of our journey is not clear.

Keep Walking on Water

During times of stress or uncertainty, we must continue to trust the journey. We must know that God will see us through whatever we are dealing with, and that He will help us to come out stronger and better in the end – even when it seems as if everything is going wrong. This is not the time to panic and sink; rather, trust that the guidance you receive from God during the calm periods will still benefit you now, even when the waters of life are choppy.

Sometimes stress stems from the inability to make a decision. Maybe your son or daughter can't decide which college to attend, when all of the options seem good. Or perhaps you've been presented with a tempting promotion at work, but it would involve more travel than you'd like. Or maybe you're experiencing difficulties with a relationship, and you don't know if it's best for both of you to end things – or if it will be worth it, in the long run, to work through it together.

Fork in the Road: Career Decisions

Years ago, I was faced with some difficult career decisions. I had already decided that I was going to exit the military and find a civilian job, but how and when to do this were not clear. I had already been on so many deployments, and I was set to be deployed again in 5 months, so I knew I needed to do something before that time – but it wasn't easy. In fact, I was about 99% certain I was going to be offered another promotion. But that would mean I couldn't return to Fort Campbell, where my family was located. At the time, my children were in 8th and 11th grades, and I did not want to relocate them to one of the five postings that would be offered.

So I took a chance, even though I wasn't sure where my next steps would lead me. I made my petition to God that I wanted to get out of the military and get into the federal job market – even though this is very difficult to do. My wife already knew this, as she had worked in a federal job that took her a very long time to break into. Getting a federal offer can take many months or years, and I only had a few months – and didn't want to miss a beat!

Wouldn't you know, I got my first federal job offer on the very same day that I officially retired from the military! As I reflected on my earlier petitions to God, I realized it was His hand that allowed these amazing events to occur in that short time. My wife later told me that she thought I was out of my mind. She said, "I can't believe it! You just thought you were going to come in and get a job just like that..."

Now, that wasn't the end of the story. While I trusted the journey and it led me to my new position, that was not the final destination for me. After some time, I realized that I was chasing money more than settling into a new career in a location that was the best for my family and me. I realized I wasn't really happy. Because things had happened so quickly following my departure from the military, I had never had a chance to breathe during that trying time.

I was commuting from Clarksville, Tennessee, to my place of work for several months. While the drive was exactly 150 miles each way from our home, my family was scattered: my daughter was in an apartment, attending her last year of college at Middle Tennessee State University, and my son was living in an apartment at the University of

Tennessee. Meanwhile, my wife was living in our 4,000 square-foot home, and I was spending nights in an apartment.

Eventually, it wore me down, and for an entire week I couldn't sleep. Something inside me said, "Hey, where's the leadership?" My family was all over the state, and I felt like it was because I was too busy chasing all these material things which I didn't really need. So I was faced with another decision: do I stay in this job, or resign? Once again, I put my trust in God to lead me to the best outcome.

I decided to resign from the Missile Defense Agency. Now, fast-forward 32 months, when I finished my Master's degree, applied for federal jobs, and received five opportunities at once! Although that was amazing, I still turned them down because I knew they weren't the right positions for me; the locations weren't right, and the positions were going to make me feel like I was back in the military.

Following my instincts paid off. Shortly thereafter, I received five more offers. This time they were all in Alabama, and I accepted one of them. The position I accepted would involve working at Army Contracting Command in Redstone Arsenal, which is in the Huntsville, Alabama area. This time, I would be working as a Contract Specialist, with the hopes of becoming a Contracting Officer (KO). I took this job, because by that point my wife was in agreement. I knew it was the right choice, because when I said yes to that job it felt like this was destiny. I knew this was the right place.

I knew it was the right choice because I'm a guy who likes to pray – especially when what I need to pray about might impact my family. I pray to God and ask Him to help me make the right decision. Earlier in my career, I received great advice from one of my commanders. There was a time when I was going to take an assignment that was going to cause me to separate from my wife. That commander said, "No, we're going to get you an assignment where your family can be together, because families are meant to be together." That has always stayed with me.

So when I was receiving all these job offers, I prayed and asked God, "Let this decision not be up to me." I had already established a career, and I didn't want to make it about me; I wanted my wife to have a say, and I wanted her to agree without my trying to manipulate her into doing what I desired to do.

Before I accepted that position, I recall my wife saying, "You know what? Let's make that move." And she said it with such a glow on her face, so it was a confirmation to me that this was the right decision.

Even though it was initially a rough transition for my wife, since for 17 years we had been in Clarksville, Tennessee, she now says it was the best move we ever made. There have been so many good things that have happened in her life that would not have occurred had we not moved. For instance, the day they were picking up my things to move here, she received a job offer in Huntsville. She hadn't been planning to move out that quickly, but this was just one more confirmation that we had made the right decision. Better yet, after we moved, she had the opportunity to go back to school and finish her degree!

Now we get to see our children more, and everything has worked out perfectly for us. For the next two years, I will get a promotion each year. After that I will be groomed for the position of Contracting Officer. This is the type of position that usually takes 10 years to earn, and I am going to earn it in three.

Most importantly, we found a good church home, so we could worship and serve in a way that is meaningful for us and that glorifies God. Trusting the journey – by "letting go and letting God" – has paid off for us financially, relationship-wise, and spiritually.

What is Your Fork in the Road?

No matter what fork in the road you face, trust that you are equipped to make the right choice. One of the easiest ways to work through the process is to leave it in God's hands. What I mean by that is to offer your prayers up to God.

Find some quiet time each day, and ask Him to show you the way. Ask Him to make it clear what you should do, and trust those intuitive feelings and ideas you receive. If you are quiet and really "listen," you will begin to get a sense of the best option for your situation.

If you try to rely on logic and rationalizations, you may inadvertently miss the messages from God. While staying grounded and practical is important, don't let that be the only deciding factor. Sometimes, the journey that is custom-made for you defies all logic – and despite that, the choice will lead you to more happiness and fulfillment than you can imagine.

Most importantly, never be afraid of failing, even when things don't turn out the way you are hoping. People often stop before achieving success because they equate failing at something with being a failure, when failing should be looked at as something that has exposed you to new possibilities. Stepping out means getting out of the familiar. Regardless of that path you take, you must always trust the journey. You need to have faith that the outcome you are seeking will be on the path you have decided to take for your journey.

Remember the words of Nelson Mandela: "I learned that courage was not the absence of fear, but the triumph over it. The brave man is not the one who does not feel afraid, but he who conquers that fear."

Worth Discussion

Just because you cannot see the fork in the road five miles ahead of you doesn't mean it is not there. In life, you are going to be required to make choices. You will need to decide which road you will travel. And because you are not privy to the result in advance, you need to trust the journey that God has prepared for you. You must remain honest and focused on your destiny, which will require you to step out of your comfort zone. It is a simple fact that life will present you with stresses and challenges; being prepared for each opportunity and becoming comfortable with trusting God is the only way to make the best decisions in your life.

In the Bible, when God asked Abraham to offer his son, Isaac, as an offering, Abraham was faced with the choice no parent would ever want to make. But through his trust in the Lord, Abraham readied his son for the offering, and in the last moment an angel stopped him from carrying out the task. Because he trusted God, Abraham did not need to follow through with an unthinkable act, and God rewarded Abraham for his faithfulness, promising him that God would bless him and his descendants as a result of his obedience.

Now, ask yourself: What decision am I facing now that requires me to put my trust in God?

CHAPTER 5

How Do I Handle My Mistakes?

The weak can never forgive.
Forgiveness is the attribute of the strong.

~ MAHATMA GANDHI

A person who denies failing at something will never achieve greatness. But if he admits and repents of those mistakes, he is granted another opportunity – if not many other opportunities. It is easy to play the blame game, but instead of blaming others, use that mistake as a lesson in life that will not let anyone stand in the way from your purpose and goals.

Finding Forgiveness

The best way to move forward after you make a mistake is to forgive yourself. At first glance, this may sound incredibly simple, yet forgiving one's self is much more difficult than it seems. For some reason, we have a hard time allowing ourselves to move on after we make a mistake – especially when that mistake hurts other people. Yes, there may be consequences that you need to face, but even so, you can forgive yourself – and God most certainly forgives you.

For example, the teenage son who took the car without permission and got into an accident made a mistake. His parents may be furious, and he might lose his driving privileges for some time, but he doesn't need to hold it against himself forever. Even if his parents don't let it go and harp on what he did wrong for months on end, that doesn't mean he can't forgive himself, do better next time, and move on.

Often I'll read in the Bible where God has forgiven our sins. In fact, when God forgives us, he forgives completely! No grudges, and no dredging up the past. When you don't allow yourself to accept that forgiveness, that is Satan's attempt to keep you mired in the mindset that you are wrong, bad, not good enough – and those thoughts will forever separate you from the wishes God has for you in your life.

As human beings, we're the ones who want to continue to hold onto that guilt. With faith and trust, however, we can break free from the shackles of guilt and shame and move onto a better phase in our lives. It says in the Bible that those who worship God must worship Him in spirit and in truth. You have to consistently be committed to believing God and His word; regardless of the situation, you cannot let those guilty thoughts and feelings take root in your mind or heart to prevent you from forgiving yourself.

I have a prayer that I pray: "God, forgive me for the things that I have done that were contrary to Your word, knowingly or unknowingly." Sometimes we are doing things that we know are wrong, but other times we may be doing things that are wrong – but we've been doing them wrong for so long that we don't see the error in our ways! Yes, we are imperfect beings in an imperfect world, trying to do the will of Someone who is perfect.

Know your worth. Maybe you don't feel worthy of receiving certain things, people, or circumstances in life, but realize that you are part of God's creation. That means that God has created you, me, and everyone on this earth for a purpose.

All things work together for the good that are called by God according to His purpose. Look for the positive, even when it appears to be a negative situation.

The Value of Adversity

When we become stressed and depressed, we are dealing with the terrible things that are happening around us, in the world, and in our lives. Sometimes we don't know what right looks like. We forget to be ourselves, and instead try to live someone else's life or do what we think others expect of us, and we make it hard on ourselves. We get down on ourselves.

It makes no difference if we have made a mistake or if life just hasn't delivered what we wanted. Either way, realize that there is value in everything you are going through. Of course, it's no fun to make a mistake. It will make you uncomfortable, especially if others are aware of your mistake. But when you move past it, many times you can use the lessons you've learned to avoid the same mistake in the future – and this will make you a better, stronger person than if you had never made the mistake in the first place.

The same goes for other uncomfortable situations you may have experienced in life. While you may not have directly brought those circumstances upon yourself, you may be living with the consequences of other people's actions or inaction. Maybe other people made mistakes that eventually took a toll on you and your life.

For example, my biological father left my mother, and I would consider that a terrible mistake that he made. It created a difficult situation for me, being part of such a large family with only our mother to provide for us. Growing up, I constantly experienced discomfort by comparing my life with the lives of those around me. I would look at the other kids in the neighborhood who appeared to be in a better place, and I would feel badly about where I was.

The two things that bothered me the most were seeing others' material advantages, and those who came from a strong, two-parent family. I had neither of those things in my life, and I wished I could have them. Many times, I would focus on the "wants" I saw around me – the new bike, the new clothes, etc. In my family, we mostly got second-hand stuff – or when we received brand-new sneakers or a cool electronic gadget, it was typically way after the fad had worn off.

Somehow, I knew deep down that I shouldn't be so selfish to think I was the one who should get everything, while I had ten siblings. With maturity, I realize that these uncomfortable experiences, as well as mistakes that I made along the way, formed the core values in my life, because now I plan ahead so I can always provide for my family. I don't want them to feel deprived, so I want to be in the position to give them things when they want them.

As a kid, I had no idea how valuable that experience would be in making me the planner and provider that I am now, but I'm glad it did! For example, my son got into an accident and couldn't drive his car, so I let him use my truck. I didn't just go out and purchase him a new car right away, but I did rent some wheels for him, and I will eventually get him another car – and I am glad I am in the position that I can do that for him.

Realizing the struggle my mother must have gone through to string things together the way she did makes me appreciate what I can give my children, and I believe that if I serve as a model for my kids the way my mom was a model for me, then they will learn lessons that will better serve them in their lives.

However, I didn't instantly pick up those lessons from my mother. I first had to learn some lessons the hard way by making some mistakes myself. For example, when I first entered the military at age 18, my first assignment was to spend two years in Germany. I quickly started living a life I wasn't used to, but because I had a place to live – three meals and a cot, as they say – and I was getting some real nice money at the same time, I felt I could spend it as I saw fit. That whole year, I spent with abandon and didn't save a single cent!

I was going out and spending money as quickly as I earned it. Luckily, I paused after that first year and said, "Wait. This isn't right." For the second year in Germany, I saved half of my monthly paycheck, and after a year of saving I finally saw the value of this practice.

I can use those financial blunders, coupled with the knowledge of my mother's frugality, to serve as a role model for my own children. At an early age, I opened bank accounts for my kids and gave them money so they could learn how to manage it. I didn't want them to grow up, make some money, and then just blow it away. I wanted them to understand the value of that money so they could be proper stewards of it. While they may make some mistakes along the way, as I did, my hope is that they will take those lessons, along with the lessons I try to instill in them, to eventually make sound choices for themselves and their future families.

Worth Discussion

Everyone makes mistakes; no one is immune! Maybe you said things to your child that you regret. Perhaps you took the credit for something you didn't do. Or maybe you lied about something so you wouldn't face the consequences. No matter how big or small the mistake, God will forgive you – but you need to forgive yourself, too!

So, ask yourself: What mistakes have I made that I need to forgive myself for? What can I learn from each mistake so I can become a better person?

CHAPTER 6

Can I Really Overcome
These Challenges?

A dream doesn't become reality through magic;
it takes sweat, determination and hard work.

~ COLIN POWELL

Is life really worth living? This was just one of the questions I pondered on a bleak December day as I seriously considered ending my life. At the time, I was 37 years old and had been on many deployments. The military is fast-paced, and instead of taking time to process and deal with everything I had experienced and seen – things that, thankfully, most civilians never experience or see – I just had to keep moving on. It's called "soldiering," and it's what most, if not all, of us do in the military, no matter how much heartbreak and carnage we have witnessed.

However, the soldiering was taking its toll on me.

Suddenly, it seemed as if I could no longer deal with things as

I had in the past. I couldn't control myself and, as a strong person, I found this both terrifying and frustrating. One day, a commander was talking to us, but I was so spaced out, with a blank look on my face, that I didn't even realize he was speaking to me! My relationships were suffering, too, as I could no longer connect with my wife and children in the same way I had before. I also found myself becoming agitated and angry with others, and sometimes I couldn't control my response to those angry and anxious feelings. There were even occasions where I voiced my true opinions of my superiors' leadership decisions, because I wanted to make them aware of how their decisions put us, their subordinates, in danger. Even though they may have considered my comments insubordinate, I wanted them to realize the weight of what they were doing.

Eventually, I got to the point where I questioned if life was worth living. The more I considered ending it all, the more I realized I couldn't solve this on my own. It wasn't until I saw a television commercial describing the symptoms of post-traumatic stress disorder that I realized that what I was experiencing actually had a name. As I listened to the announcer in the commercial, I felt like he was describing me!

When I was first diagnosed with PTSD, I didn't want to admit it to anyone else. I thought, "Why do I need to go get help to put my life back together the way it used to be?" But I soon admitted to myself that I couldn't do this alone. I simply didn't know how to put my life back together. And the thoughts of ending my life were becoming more frequent. Finally, I gave in and found help.

Looking back, it's no surprise that what I had experienced was too much to handle, between a near-death experience in Iraq and having friends who were alive and well one day and then dead the next. Fortunately, since those dark days, I have gotten the help I needed and, supported by my love for God and my family, I got past those hopeless thoughts.

I didn't want to put my family through a traumatic experience, and even in the desperate moments in which I just wanted to be free from the pain, I resolved not to do it. I knew that ending my life would cause my family immense pain and suffering, and I was not about to cause that type of hurt and trauma to the people I loved the most.

You're Not Alone

You don't need to be a vet with PTSD to get to these low points in your life. A death in the family, divorce, abuse, or other trauma can bring you to your knees. And in some cases, there is no single defining moment that causes despair: the daily stresses of life can simply accumulate and take their toll, leading some to a place of helplessness and hopelessness.

While it is normal to experience some of these negative feelings in your life, you don't need to remain there forever! Challenging relationships or circumstances in life can be overcome – even when the odds appear to be stacked against you.

In my case, it was my faith, the professional counseling, and support from my wife that helped me to move beyond the PTSD and get back on my feet. While there are still times that I cannot watch certain television shows because they might bring me back to a dark place, I have learned how to deal with those situations that have the potential to cause me to backslide. Most importantly, it was my determination and perseverance that saw me through those difficulties.

Determined

Once you have envisioned your dream, then you must find a way to pursue it. Don't let life's challenges or difficult people distract you or cause you to lose faith. Some people go around mountains, while some people simply choose to climb mountains; whichever method you choose, you will eventually conquer the mountain if you do not give in, tire, or simply quit. In other words, you must be determined.

I remember my mother doing so much with so little in the way of resources. How did she do it? Through unwavering determination and her desire to provide for us. While we did not always get what the other kids in the neighborhood and school got, what we did receive on a constant basis was the love of our mother. There is nothing better than a mother's love – a love reflected through her actions, from waiting for the next welfare check to feed us to making sure we had clean clothes for school. I do know that throughout each challenge and hardship, she trusted in God and kept her faith in Him.

When Jesus fed the five thousand with two fish and five loaves of bread, He was determined to provide for many with limited resources. My mother did the same. There were many summers spent playing with cousins in the project, or walking two miles to the nearest store to pass the time. Meanwhile, my classmates were taking vacations with their parents or visiting relatives in other cities and states. Yes, I envied the luxuries that I knew we couldn't afford, yet through it all, I knew my mother was doing the best she could. My mother, in her determination, continued to provide for us, and at the same time I remained determined: I never gave up on my dream that someday I would be able to have experiences that the other kids experienced – even though I couldn't see a way during my childhood.

Finding Your Way

You must find a way to pursue your dreams, and the first thing you need to do is remain focused. Instead of allowing distractions, people, or circumstances to slow you down, try to learn from any challenges you face, and use those lessons to continue to move toward your dream.

For example, if you're trying to start a small business, but don't have enough money for your startup, don't just give up! Maybe you have skills that others don't have, and you can provide your service for free in exchange for free advertising, website development, etc. Or perhaps you'll begin a crowd-funding campaign that fully funds your startup costs. Or maybe you'll qualify for a small business loan. My point is, when you think a roadblock is impossible to overcome, stay focused on the goal as you continue to look for ways to move past the challenge.

Next, stop making excuses for why you can't achieve your dream. Thinking you're too young, immature, inexperienced, or whatever is just making excuse instead of looking clearly at the challenges you need to overcome. Do not allow age to rob you of your future! You may think you're too old, but realize that wisdom can energize your passion. On the other hand, if you think you're too young, your youthful optimism and energy can help you make it over any bumps in the road that you encounter. Time is constantly moving, and you don't want to be left behind because you were too busy making excuses rather than paying attention to the opportunities that are already surrounding you.

Another excuse people cling to is that they can't possibly do something because they've never done it before. They have no experience. So, how can one become a trailblazer without ever walking the trail? Start by looking at the trailblazers who have gone before you and are blazing a trail with their lives today. Look for mentors and role models to follow. Read biographies to learn from others' successes and mistakes. Talk to people who are knowledgeable in your area of interest. Take courses. Network. Grow.

I am not quite where I want to be in my life, yet I am in a great place and am getting closer to my goals each day. I took on the challenges of writing this book to motivate myself to excel beyond what I thought were my limits. In this way, I have blazed my first trail (therefore making me a trailblazer!), because I will now empower readers with an opportunity to better their lives and give birth to their visions and dreams.

Not everyone will understand or appreciate what you are doing. Not everyone will be supportive. Sometimes well-intentioned people are worried you will fail, so they try to prevent you from experiencing disappointment. Others may be jealous, or fear that you are a threat to them in some way. No matter what the reason is, you don't need to let other people stop you from chasing your dream. We are created differently, and therefore we think differently. Even if someone else does not share your dream, that does not mean that your dream is wrong. It just means that we all have different goals and desires.

For these reasons, choose your friends wisely. Too many people I knew got caught up in drugs or made other poor decisions. That doesn't have to be you! You don't have to make the kinds of decisions that you're going to regret for the rest of your life.

A mistake is just that, but some people consider mistakes as failure. Just because you didn't progress for two years, it doesn't make you a failure. Maybe you made mistakes during that time; just acknowledge them and move in the right direction now. You can actually take your "failures" and reframe them as mistakes so you can use them as learning experiences.

I have learned to look for friends who remain positive and supportive, even during bad times. In my opinion, a friend is supportive if he or she prayerfully provides guidance when I'm going through a trial or remains my friend even when he or she disagrees with my decisions.

Another important aspect of a healthy friendship is the ability to strike a balance between give and take. Good friends have helped me discover the best of myself, and I help them to be their best as well. Trustworthiness and respect are two other critical qualities in a true friend. I want someone who can honestly challenge my opinion yet do so in a way that is not condescending or rude.

Through the years, I've become more discriminating in my choice of friends because I realized that there were some friends who never wanted to encourage me or hear about any of my accomplishments, achievements, or plans to do something rewarding. Instead, they would make statements meant to bring me down or cast doubt on my dreams. I like to call them "dream killers," because they would attempt to discourage me for their own selfish gain – whether the benefit for them was to feel better about themselves, perceive themselves to be superior to me, or something else. As a result, I made a conscious choice to simply avoid negative friends, and my circle of friends has become much smaller. However, those who remain in that circle are true friends for life, and that has led to a state of satisfaction and inner peace that is far more rewarding than maintaining friendships that are not genuine, supportive, or life-giving. Through solid friendships, you can see yourself through any challenges you may encounter – because your real friends will give you the strength you need, want, and deserve.

Overcoming Challenges: A True Story

By following through with the dream of writing my first book, I can serve as a model for someone else. Even if he or she does not want to become an author, a reader of this book can follow my lead and start his or her journey. You too can get on a positive path, if only you realize that you matter. What you want in life is important, and you need to believe that yourself.

To illustrate my point, I would like to share with you a major obstacle I overcame in my journey to receive a college degree. By the time I had reached my junior year in high school, I was considered an all-star in football. Colleges began recruiting me, talking to me about having the opportunity to play football at the collegiate level. As if my size wasn't challenging enough at 5'5", my mom was a widow on federal assistance, and these complications seemed to scare off the University of Pine Bluff, Arkansas. Another college that was seriously considering me, Mississippi Delta, required that I complete a tryout before making a decision, which was fine with me because I knew I had talent; however, the high school that I attended did not want to pay the insurance that the college required to complete the tryout on a college campus. Henderson State University in Arkadelphia, Arkansas, had expressed interest, but I never heard back from them after the initial contact. With my promising prospects dwindling, I graduated from high school with no scholarship or concrete plan.

While I tried to figure out what I was going to do, I hopped on a Greyhound bus to the state of Washington, where my brother was stationed at Fort Lewis. After a brief stint working at Taco Bell, I decided that military life might suit me better. I took and passed the test to join the Army Reserve, only to be blown off by an active Army recruiter. You see, he was not going to receive credit for recruiting me for the Reserves; he would only get credit if I went full-time. I explained what happened to my brother, and he told me I may as well go full-time because after basic training – which was the same for the reserve and full-time – it was just a job after that. So, I decided that I would go full-time (regular army), and off to the recruiter I went. Wouldn't you know, once I told him I was interested in going full-time, I suddenly received his undivided attention!

With everything set up, I took my physical, chose a job skill, and in 63 days I would be headed off for Basic Training. Being only 17 years old at the time, I returned home so my mother could sign off on the paperwork. Just before being shipped off to Fort Dix, New Jersey, I ran into my high school football coach.

"Congratulations!" he said. When he noticed my puzzled look, he added, "Congratulations on that football scholarship!"

Now I was really confused. I asked, "What scholarship?"

He laughed. "Quit pulling my leg. . ." He told me about the football scholarship I was offered from Henderson State University. He had sent the letter to me while I was in Tacoma, Washington.

I called my brother to verify if a letter had been sent to me at his address from the college. Indeed, Henderson State had sent a letter, and he admitted he received it months before I found out from my coach. "Why didn't you tell me?" I asked him incredulously.

He answered, "Because either you go to the Army and make money, or you can go to college and be broke."

My brother denied me the chance of attending college right out of high school, and what an awful thing for him to do in keeping my Letter of Intent from me. Not only did that prevent me from playing collegiate football but also prevented me from obtaining a higher education out of high school.

It all came down to making the decision to commit to my dreams – and not allowing friends, family, and life to stand in the way any longer. People may have attempted to keep me off the path on the way to my dreams, but I didn't need to succumb to failure after each setback. I knew I could still make my own choices in life. Even if it happened later in life than I had originally planned, I was – and still am – responsible for the decisions I make. Through unwavering commitment, I finally was able to realize my dream.

Worth Discussion

Your life is what you make of it. When you understand this principle, you will be more determined and less inclined to give up or tire out as you try to make certain milestones that are necessary for growth. Ask yourself: What challenges am I facing that will force me to persevere and remain determined?

CHAPTER 7

It's Never Too Late . . . Start Now!

The time is always right to do what is right.

~ MARTIN LUTHER KING, JR.

To realize your dreams, the most important thing is that you believe that you deserve them. Although this may sound obvious, many people unconsciously sabotage their ability to reach their goals because they don't truly believe that they deserve the accomplishment.

Know that you are a creation of God, and none of us were put on this Earth to fail; He created us in His glory, and therefore it is critical for each of us to maintain a positive outlook on life. Remind yourself that you do deserve to accomplish your goals!

Don't Follow the Crowd: Get the Crowd to Follow You!

Some people may try to prevent you from achieving your dreams. It doesn't matter if it's a relative, friend, or enemy: some folks want to see you fail, others believe they are giving you "good advice" so you don't experience disappointment, and others feel threatened by success because they have not been able to be successful themselves. Regardless of the motive, these people are not going to propel you toward your goal. You don't need to listen to them!

As I mentioned earlier, my brother thought it was in my best interests to join the Army, and he essentially blocked my chances of entering college. But I didn't let that stop me. Eventually, I took advantage of the GI Bill and got my degree. And I didn't stop there; I continued my education until I earned my MBA. What did I consider more important? Did I just try to go with the crowd? Absolutely not. Following the crowd is where so many of us go wrong. I know far too many people who just followed others' lead, had no idea who they were, and didn't realize they were going down the wrong road.

I decided to follow a different path. I wanted to be the one who inspires the crowd; I wanted to draw them in. In the words of John C. Maxwell, "A leader is one who knows the way, goes the way, and shows the way." I wanted to become that kind of leader.

I began working on my circle of influence by concentrating on those closest to me. For example, I worked to make an impact on my children – by being a positive example for them, because that was my responsibility. It wasn't easy, though, since I was trying to be a great dad without ever having the modeling of a strong father figure in my own life. But instead of giving up, I remembered the example my mother set for us kids. She wasn't a father figure, of course; but she was compassionate, empathetic, selfless, and determined to be the best provider she could be. Certainly, these are the traits of an excellent parent, whether it's a mother or a father. By following my mother's lead, I was able to show my children the way.

Next, I asked myself how I could be a better friend. Growing up, I didn't have a lot of friends outside of my cousins or other family members. Here again, I was somewhat limited, but I didn't let that stop me from learning how to be a positive, loyal, generous friend to others.

Once I realized that I could make a difference in other people's lives by influencing those closest to me, I finally possessed the confidence and courage to influence a broader circle of people. From those I encountered at work or church – and now to anyone who reads this book! – I am widening the scope of my influence and inspiration, with the hope that others will join the positive, life-giving, optimistic "crowd" that I have cultivated.

Consider how you can do the same in your life: influence those closest to you first, experience some small successes, and then broaden your horizons as you stretch the limits of your comfort zone. For example, if you have a service to offer others, begin by offering that service to friends and family. Receive honest feedback and constructive criticism, and then continue to hone your craft as you offer your service to those in your neighborhood. As success builds upon success, you can expand your reach to neighboring towns, your county, your state, and beyond. Reach for the stars, and stretch as much as you can! The more you prove to yourself that you can realize your goals, the bolder you will become in what you can accomplish.

Choose Your Crowd Wisely

When thinking about your dreams – and those you want to share your dreams with – assess those around you. Whether it is friends or family, determine who is most supportive of your goals as you pursue them, along with anyone who might not be quite so encouraging. Remember the story of Joseph? He once had a dream that his family would bow down to him. When he told his family, however, not only did they not believe him, but his brothers also plotted to have him killed – even though they eventually changed their minds and sold him into slavery instead. Fortunately, Joseph remained resilient through these hardships and challenges, and eventually he rose to a position of wealth and power in Egypt. He even forgave his brothers for their deceitful acts and became known as the father of two tribes in Israel.

Hopefully, you will never have anyone around you as dangerous as Joseph's brothers – but this story does illustrate the importance of being careful with whom you share your deepest desires and aspirations. Only share your hopes and dreams with those who will support and encourage you throughout your journey when you make yourself vulnerable to pursue your goals.

Discovering My Strengths

The next step to getting started now is to recognize your strengths and use them to your advantage. One of my strengths is being able to connect with people to make them feel good about themselves. When I was younger, I didn't realize this was a gift of mine. However, when I entered the military I found myself being given numerous leadership positions. I think other people already saw something in me that I couldn't yet see within myself. All I knew was that I always took an interest in being around older, wiser people. I had a keen interest in learning from them, and I just felt I was learning more from them – rather than always hanging around people in my age group or those who were in a similar position to me. I didn't realize this at the time, but I was learning about life through them, learning how to rise to a higher level. I never would have gotten to this point if I had just followed the crowd.

Another strength of mine is to have the willpower to see through any challenges that I may come across. I first realized this strength when I joined the military, because I was now exposed to different groups of people. I would look around and say to myself, "I can do what they do – maybe even better! – if I simply apply myself."

Knowing I wanted the good things in life, while at the same time making others feel good about themselves, gave me an inner strength to follow my dreams, no matter what. In basic training, the first contact a recruit has is with the drill sergeant. I dreamed about how I could one day become a sergeant, making a positive impact as a new recruit's first impression in the army. I even remember picking up my sergeant's hat when he had placed it on a desk in the common area during an inspection – and asking my buddy to snap a quick picture of me wearing the hat, for a little bit of motivation! By tapping into my inner strength to persevere long enough, I eventually was able to become a drill sergeant, one of the proudest achievements of my life.

One of my other strengths is the ability to inspire people spiritually. That started when I came home from the Republic of South Korea, and my pastor would just captivate me with his stories. I loved how he knew the Bible in a way that allowed him to describe the practical applications of the Scriptures to my life. This inspired me to work in different areas of the ministry, from usher to media to brotherhood president. Over time, a feeling came over me that was so spiritual in nature that I knew it had to come from God. It was my call to enter the ministry. When I first felt the call, I didn't tell anyone – not even my wife. I didn't want anyone to influence me one way or the other. When I did share what I was thinking with her, she immediately said, "Oh, yeah. I think you should do it."

Initially, I didn't even want to do it, yet something just kept pulling me. It was not a want – it was this indescribable need to get into that area. One day I was talking to my brother, and he said, "You sound different." So I went to my pastor to sort through these feelings, and he handed me a packet, saying, "I think you need to take this. Just listening to what you're saying, I think you need to take this and fill it out." It was an application for a minister's license.

I completed the packet and the training, and the day I delivered my first sermon, I just felt so good about it! Public speaking would become one of my strengths as well, knowing that I can look out at the crowd and capture their attention with a thought-provoking question. To this day, it sometimes blows my mind that everything I was absorbing earlier in life I was actually learning from and would apply in my ministry.

My wife says my strengths have blossomed because I have a compassion for people and a strong desire to get them to the point where they can excel in life or get to that place where they feel comfortable in their lives and encouraged. Others have said it is my people skills, my ability to walk in confidence, and learn quickly – combined with being trustworthy, disciplined, honest and ambitious. Most likely, the reason I feel so passionate about what I am doing is due to the fact that the strengths I can acknowledge today are the same areas that I felt were missing from my life. Interestingly, many of those strengths were there all along!

Discovering Your Strengths

You've read about my strengths, but what about yours? What gifts, talents, and skills do you have that will propel you on the path toward your dreams?

Before you dismiss this section or argue that you have no strengths, think again! It may be cliché, but remember, "God doesn't make junk." It's true that the Almighty Creator blessed you with gifts that you can use to experience success and help others.

Consider your interpersonal skills, physical attributes, technical skills, emotional intelligence, educational level, background experiences (both good and bad), the people you know, and topics that interest you. All of these areas may point to your personal set of strengths that you bring to this world. Also consider compliments you've received in the past. What have people told you that you are good at? These comments can certainly reveal some of your talents and skills.

Even certain criticisms can hint at a strength of yours. For example, if someone says you're stubborn, turn it around: there's a good chance you are resilient and determined – and not one to give up or give in easily. What about the criticism that you're too emotional? Flip the script and realize that you may have deep compassion and empathy for people and causes that are important to you. Or what if someone has pegged you as one who likes to argue? Maybe that rational-logical nature of yours can be used to persuade and sway others in a positive direction.

As you begin to identify your strengths, write them down and post them in a location you will see frequently. This will help build your confidence, remind you that you are someone with unique talents, and serve as a motivator to remain focused in pursuit of your goals and dreams.

Speaking of goals and dreams, be sure you identify your goals. If you don't, you won't know if you achieved any success. That's why goal setting in life is so important; even if others witness your success, you may not recognize it if you never determined your goals with clarity. If you need help getting started with goal setting, check out the study guides for chapter 7 in the back of the book for more guidance and support.

Leveling Up

As I mentioned, my life was not always easy, especially during my earlier years. However, I did not allow this to deprive me of things I wanted to achieve. In fact, the challenges of my upbringing motivated me to work even harder to achieve new levels of success. I use the word "level," because each time you feel that you have achieved success, you'll find that success never stops. There will always be another level of success that you will strive for once you reach a milestone or goal.

For instance, every time I worked toward a position in the military, I would end up getting that position. But instead of being content with that stage, I would look ahead to the next position, and eventually I would get promoted to that level. This is how I went from being a sergeant first class (an instructor with high achievement) to drill sergeant with high achievement to warrant officer with high achievement.

I always looked for the next rung on the ladder. Now, this doesn't mean that I was unhappy with each promotion. On the contrary; I was grateful for the opportunities. But at the same time I knew there was even more out there for me to experience. I would say, "I'm here right now. Where do I go next?" I knew that even if I appeared to be the most experienced compared with those around me, there was a good chance there was someone with the same skill set in another state. So I needed to position myself for any and all potential competition, which led me to the next question: "What have I done to stand out?" Just because I got to a certain point, I knew that someone else in another part of the country must have gotten to that point as well.

In writing this book, I feel as if I'm standing on the shoulders of the giants who have gone before me. I look at someone like TD Jakes (one of America's best known preachers) and see a person who started out in the hills of West Virginia with a tiny congregation – and look at the millions of people whose lives he has touched today! I stand on someone's shoulders like him and learn by his example so that I, too, can make a profound impact in others' lives.

You can do the same in your life. Everyone is looking for someone to help motivate him or her. Give that person guidance, and be a leader in his or her life. Whatever point you're at in your life, you can be that inspiration to others and still look forward to even higher levels of success as you achieve your goals.

Worth Discussion

Whatever you want to accomplish in life, be sure to believe that you have the ability to accomplish it. Also believe that you deserve to realize your dreams. As you consider your strengths and goals, answer these questions: What are my strengths? What steps can I take to accomplish my goals? What can I do to get started today?

CHAPTER 8

Your Heart Holds the Key
to Your Purpose

The best and most beautiful things in the world
cannot be seen or even touched — they
must be felt with the heart.

~ HELEN KELLER

Living With an Eternal Perspective

This life we are living is much more spiritual than natural, and as you begin to understand this fact, you will be fully equipped to rise above the noise and view everything with a better perspective. You are a creation of God, and knowing that alone should be enough to assure you that you are deserving of so much more.

When you view life from a spiritual perspective, as God intended, you can begin living with an "eternal perspective." The word of God, John 4:24, lets us know that "God is a spirit, and his worshipers must worship in the spirit and in truth" (NIV). For this reason, do not allow the natural things in life to consume you, as though that is all life has to offer. Life is made up of much more than the riches in the world and material things that we desire. An eternal perspective involves seeing the world the way God desires for us to view everything; that is how we find peace and build a relationship with God. That is how we impact and influence the lives of others to make the world that we live in as God intended – with love and unity.

To live life with that eternal perspective, it is critical to realize that we were created to serve and not to be served. That is true power! Society has caused people to believe that having power means obtaining a lot of money, being at the top of a career, or owning big houses and nice cars. While there is nothing wrong with having those things, it becomes problematic when you lose yourself in material items. Instead, we need to live with the mindset that we are servants. Although at first glance this may sound difficult or unappealing, the reverse is true; living a life in service to others is actually the most fulfilling way to live!

Heart Over Matter

Jesus was the perfect example of what it means to serve and not be served. We should love God more than the love of the accumulation of things here on earth. The heart is more important than the material things of this world, and if you don't believe that, just consider anyone you know who has died. He or she could not take anything along with him or her after death. Even when we are alive, it is easy to gain – or lose – material things. Maybe you have inherited something, or maybe you have earned it. Either way, realize that nothing is guaranteed and it is quite possible to lose everything in the blink of an eye.

However, when you stand before God, if you have put His priorities over your own, God will recognize that you have been a good and faithful servant. This is what I mean by "heart over matter." It means that you have put your spiritual heart – one that follows God and his messages – over your own desires for stuff, status, and sensory thrills.

Nothing that you do or accumulate in life matters if the heart of what you do is not on the Glory of God. When God has entrusted you with things or allowed you to accumulate things, it is for you – but not just for you alone. When God gives you something, He has entrusted you to be a good steward of that gift, whether it be something material, a talent, or a skill. He wants you to use what you have been given to encourage and empower others, and to win souls for Him.

Putting Heart Over Matter Into Action

One simple way to begin putting heart over matter is to stop living your life based on what other people expect or demand of you. Instead, start living a life that meets God's expectations for you. Mark 12:30 (NIV) put it this way: "Love the Lord your God with all your heart and with all your soul and with all your mind and with all your strength." Although people will require many things from you, God only asks for one thing: that you love Him with your whole being.

My mother was a prime example of loving God with her whole being, and sharing that love through her service to others. She not only did everything in her power to provide for our family, but she also served as a role model and teacher who tried to influence her children and encourage them to live Godly lives.

In addition to loving God, you also need to surrender to His will. How can you accomplish this? By realizing that it is God who grants you your abilities. The sooner you realize and recognize that your talents and gifts are not of your own making, the more quickly you will find your strength in Jesus.

The good news is that once you surrender to this fact, you can replace the temporal happiness in this world with joy, which is eternal. Happiness is fleeting, experienced by moments of comfort, material accumulation, worldly successes, and the like. Living a life with joy, on the other hand, is where you will find your strength and open yourself up to the opportunities that God places in front of you. It doesn't mean you are always in a state of bliss, but it does mean that you will feel deep contentment and "the peace of God, which passeth all understanding" (Philippians 4:7, KJV).

When my mom passed away on September 7, 2015, I found myself doing something that had never crossed my mind – and that was to conduct her eulogy. Matthew 22:14 states, "For many are called, but few are chosen." God chose me, and once I trusted in God to give me the strength to follow through and deliver the eulogy – despite my fears – I was able to communicate to everyone who came to her funeral the amazing woman that she was. Through that eulogy, I allowed her memory to live on by highlighting the legacy she left in this world.

When I accepted the call to give her eulogy, I found that I was open to accepting the call into ministry as well. I never imagined that

God would choose me for such an awesome responsibility, but I am glad that I had an ear to not only hear Him but also to accept His call – and that call has filled my heart with more joy than anything the natural world could ever offer.

When Man Says No, God Says Yes

You must not allow anyone or anything to keep you from giving birth to your dreams. You have to believe the report of Jesus. In other words, you must pay attention to the plan that God has for your life – not what other people may think they have planned for you. If I had given up whenever someone else told me no, I would also have given up on the things that God desired for me: to empower others to believe they are capable of accomplishing anything they put they mind to – if they would just believe.

When I served in the United States Army, I wanted to become a Warrant Officer, only to be told no by the Senior Warrant Officer over the Regimental Corps at the time. However, before the final decision was made, I got my hopes up. The officer had personally called me to say that I had a great packet and would actually get selected if he approved that my packet go before the board. In that same call, he also mentioned that he preferred a particular skill set (that was not a requirement). Even though I met all of the qualifications that were in place at the time, the officer did not select me. But I did not give up.

Following that disappointment, I went on to accomplish another dream, that of becoming a Drill Sergeant. At the end of my time as a Drill Sergeant, I resubmitted my packet in hopes of becoming a Warrant Officer at last. By this time, the personnel of the

Senior Warrant Officer for the Regimental Corp for ordinance had changed. I decided to get on the calendar and have a meeting with the new Senior Warrant Officer to explain how the previous officer did not allow my packet to go before the board for consideration.

Fortunately, this officer saw things from my perspective and asked me to resubmit my packet to the board, which was to take place within a matter of weeks. I resubmitted and called to verify his receipt of the packet. The officer confirmed that he received my packet, and went on to tell me that it was an outstanding packet that he would be happy to send to the board. Ultimately, I was selected by the panel to be accepted into the Warrant Officer Corp. To God be the glory!

If I had listened to what the first officer told me, I would have accepted "no" as the final answer. Instead, I trusted that when man says no, God says yes, and today I can proudly say that I retired from the United States Army as a Warrant Officer.

But the story doesn't end there because on my official retirement date, I was offered a position with the federal government. Because I adhered to the Word of God, He allowed me to triumph over the decisions of man and placed me in a position to retire with honors and even go on to be accepted into a federal government position.

My hope for you is that you begin to believe the report of God rather than the report of man; in this way, you will receive those things that God desires for you. Never have these words been more true: "Seek ye first the Kingdom of God and His righteousness: and all of these things shall be added unto you" (Matthew 6:33, KJV).

Worth Discussion

God wants us to love Him with all our hearts. He also wants us to surrender and acknowledge that everything we have been given comes from Him. This means that we need to put our life's purpose into action in a way that serves God and others. Rather than worrying about worldly success and wealth, keep your eye focused on the intentions that God has placed within your heart. When you follow God's plan for your life, you will not only notice Him opening more doors for you, but you will also experience a deep sense of joy and contentment. As you think about your life's purpose, ask yourself this question: What is the greater purpose I will fulfill by putting "heart over matter" to achieve my goals?

STUDY GUIDES

STUDY GUIDE

Chapter One

What is Real Success?

In this chapter, you discovered that, while it is easy to think that others may be "ahead" of you in life, that is usually not the case at all. Everyone struggles. Everyone has moments of doubt. However, it is not easy to remain confident, especially when society bombards us with a false definition of success that leads to even more self-doubt.

To prevent yourself from being intimidated by others' successes, keep your eye focused on the most important kind of success: Godly success. Following through what God desires for your life will ultimately result in success after success – even during challenging times.

To understand this point more fully, I suggest you read Genesis 39:1-23. After you read the story of Joseph and Potiphar's wife, continue reading below and answer the questions with your discussion group.

Questions for Adult Groups

Despite being tempted by Potiphar's wife, Joseph refused to sin against God and give in to her propositions. And while this refusal resulted in his being thrown in prison, it is important to note that this setback did not slow down God's blessings. Even in prison, God made sure that Joseph was recognized and given a special position – because he followed God's plan for his life, God rewarded Joseph for that loyalty.

1. What kinds of temptations have you faced at work? At home? Among your friends?

2. If you gave in to the temptation, what was the result, and how do you believe this impacted your ability to experience Godly success?

3. If you resisted the temptation, how has God granted blessings in your life?

4. Consider a time when you were tempted to follow worldly success (money, fame, power, etc.). How does this contradict what God wants for your life?

5. How often do you compare yourself with others and measure your level of success against them? If God could speak to you right now, what advice do you believe He would offer?

6. Think back to other times you have been rewarded by God for following His will. Discuss with the group how this translates into "Godly success."

Questions for Teens

While Potiphar was away from home, his wife tried to seduce Joseph. Even though Joseph did the right thing by refusing, Potiphar's wife lied and accused Joseph of trying to take advantage of her. This led to Joseph being thrown into jail. Fortunately, even jail did not stop God from blessing Joseph. God helped the jail warden recognize Joseph's talents, and over time Joseph was put in charge of others in the prison. Joseph did not let temptations and society's standards of "success" influence him. Instead, Joseph was able to experience Godly success in his life through his faithfulness and loyalty to God.

1. Teens and young adults face all kinds of temptations. Sometimes, those temptations are serious, ranging from things like cheating or stealing to getting involved with drugs and alcohol. Other times, the temptations seem trivial, like engaging in gossip, making fun of the new kid, or telling a white lie to parents or teachers to avoid getting in trouble. What kinds of temptations have you faced at school or work? At home with your family? When you're hanging out with friends?

2. Think about a time when you gave in to the temptation. What was the result? In what way may this have prevented you from experiencing God's blessings?

3. Now think back to a time that you resisted the temptation. How did God grant blessings in your life?

4. Our society considers those with lots of money, power,

or popularity as the most successful people. Think back to a time when you were tempted to follow this definition of success. How does this contradict what God might want for your life?

5. Look at anyone's Instagram account, and it's easy to feel like you don't measure up. How often do you compare yourself with others and measure your level of success against them? If God could speak to you right now, what advice do you believe He would offer?

6. Think back to other times you have been rewarded by God for following His will. Discuss with the group how this translates into "Godly success."

STUDY GUIDE

Chapter Two

The Importance of You

There is a story within you – and it is important for you to *believe* that your story is worth sharing! While fear may tempt you into thinking you don't have anything to offer the world, realize that the self-doubt is simply an illusion that keeps you separated from your true purpose.

By exploring your talents and acknowledging your strengths, you too can build a stronger personal identity – and ultimately share the best of yourself with those around you.

Matthew 25:14-30 illustrates these points poignantly. After reading the parable of the talents, reflect on the questions below and then discuss your thoughts with the group.

Questions for Adult Groups

In this story, the three servants received money (talents) from their master and made decisions about how to handle the money that had been entrusted to them. While two of the men traded the money in order to make even more for their master, the last servant fearfully hid the money and simply returned the original sum. Not only did the master reward the first two servants, but he also chastised the third servant for living in fear and not making the most of what was given to him.

Whether it's money, a certain skill set, specific personality traits, intelligence, or some other quality, each one of us has been given special talents from God. No matter how significant or small you may think your talents are, God expects you to use what you have been given to the fullest.

1. What talents has God given you? If you find it difficult to identify your talents, ask others in the group to share what they view as your talents. Their answers may pleasantly surprise you!

2. How have you let fear get in the way of acknowledging and using your talents to the fullest? Give an example; what held you back?

3. What choices have you made that allow your talents to shine?

4. What choices have you made that obscure your talents?

5. Consider how your talents and skills may relate to the purpose God has for your life. If you are unsure, ask other people in your discussion group to help you brainstorm ways to use your talents. (Note: If you are still uncertain about your life purpose at this point, the study guide for the next chapter will assist you further.)

Questions for Teens

In this story, three servants received money from their master and made decisions about how to handle what he gave them. Two of the men doubled the amount they had been given, while the last servant fearfully hid his money, returning the original bag of gold to the master upon his return. While the master rewarded the two enterprising servants, he criticized the one who lived in fear and did nothing with his money.

In a similar way, God has granted you specific talents. Maybe you're a talented public speaker or have an incredible sense of humor. Or perhaps you're an excellent student, musician, or artist. Maybe you can empathize with others – or maybe you are a good listener. No matter how big or small you may believe your talents to be, realize that God wants you to use what you have been given to the fullest.

1. What talents has God given you? If you find it difficult to identify your talents, ask around. Your friends might see things in you that you don't even recognize in yourself!

2. How have you let fear get in the way of appreciating your talents and using them to the fullest?

3. Think back to a time when you were proud of one of your talents. How did you let your talent shine?

4. Have you ever tried to hide a talent – or refused to admit that you had any talent? If so, discuss how that made you feel.

5. How might your strengths relate to the purpose God has for your life? If you are unsure, ask those in your discussion group to help you brainstorm ways you might begin to apply your talents toward your life's purpose. (Note: If you are still uncertain about your life purpose, there's no need to worry! The study guide for Chapter Three will guide you further.)

STUDY GUIDE

Chapter Three

The Secret to Finding Your Destiny

In this section we'll continue exploring how you can use your God-given gifts to the best of your ability to identify your true purpose in this world.

Just as everyone has his or her own special combination of talents, the purpose God has for your life is unique to you as well. That's why you should stop comparing yourself to others: someone else's path is not necessarily the one you are meant to follow.

As you become more confident in your abilities, you will need to step out of your comfort zone – and that can be scary! The best way to deal with those fears is to turn over your insecurities and doubts to God. He is the one who can give you the strength and wisdom you need to succeed and follow through with whatever God has put in your heart.

I suggest you turn to Acts 9:10-19. This story will both

reinforce the concepts presented in this chapter and prepare you to answer the following questions:

Questions for Adult Groups

How scared Ananias must have been when God tasked him with healing Saul! As a well-known persecutor of Christians, Saul would have been the last person Ananias, a God-fearing Christian, would want to visit. But Ananias accepted his talent as a healer, put his trust in God, and listened to what God put within his heart. By following God's will, Ananias healed Saul and opened the door for Saul's surprising conversion to Christianity.

1. Now that you have considered your talents from Chapter Two, take time to think about how God wants you to use your talents. How can these talents be used in your life? Do they help point you to your purpose?

2. What is your purpose? Take some quiet time to reflect on and reaffirm what God has put into your heart. Share this with the group, and prayerfully ask them to support and encourage you, especially when any fears may get in your way.

3. If you have not yet determined your purpose, you may need to understand the fears that may be holding you back. For example, if you know you are talented at public speaking – but fear you have nothing powerful to say – your fear of not having an important message may be

an obstacle. What fears and obstacles may be blocking you from your destiny? Discuss your discoveries with the group.

4. What can you do today to move yourself out of your comfort zone – and one step closer to your purpose? Share your ideas with the group (or ask for help on this one if you're not sure of possible next steps).

Questions for Teens

Everyone knew that Saul of Tarsus hated Christians. So imagine how scared Ananias must have been when God chose him to use his talent as a healer to help Saul! Although he was fearful, Ananias followed God's direction and restored Saul's eyesight. This powerful experience ultimately led to Saul's conversion – and this new Christian (later known as Paul) became one of the most influential men in Christian history! Ananias's willingness to step out of his comfort zone and realize his purpose made a powerful and important contribution to Christianity.

1. What are some of the talents you identified from Chapter Two? As you reflect on your talents, think about how God may want you to use them to fulfill your life's purpose. Discuss your findings with the group.

2. What is your purpose? Take some quiet time to reaffirm what God has put into your heart. Share your thoughts

with the group, and prayerfully ask them to support and encourage you, especially when fear creeps in.

3. If you still aren't sure what your purpose is, take some time to consider the fears that may be holding you back. For example, if you know you are a creative artist – but everyone tells you that you can never make a living as an artist – you may be letting other people's opinions get in your way. What fears and obstacles may be blocking you from your destiny? Discuss your discoveries with the group.

4. What can you do today to move yourself out of your comfort zone – and one step closer to your purpose? Share your ideas with the group (or ask for help on this one if you're stuck).

Study Guide

Chapter Four

Trust the Journey

In life you will face difficult decisions, whether at home, school, work, or in relationships. Sometimes, the path is clear, and you will know exactly what to do. At other times, there will be a clear "fork" in the road – but the choice will not be so easy. If each option leads to both positive and negative consequences, making a choice may be difficult. And sometimes your conscience may be pulling you in one direction, based on "the right thing to do" – but there may be another side of you that wants to head in a different direction.

When facing these difficult decisions, be sure that you turn to God. He will guide you every step of the way – if you let Him. Chapters 13 and 14 in the book of Numbers show the sort of difficult choices the Israelites faced. I suggest you read this story to learn more about their struggles, as well as how they handled their difficult fork in the road.

Questions for Adult Groups

God planned to give the land of Canaan to the Israelites, but He first asked Moses to send men into the land and then report their findings to the group. The report filled many with fear: although the land was fertile, those who currently inhabited Canaan were large and powerful, with fortified cities that would be difficult to attack.

Hearing this, most of the Israelites wanted to back down – but not Joshua or Caleb. They both trusted the Lord and had faith in Him. Joshua asked the others to trust God and not be afraid, but few listened. As a result, of that group of leaders only Joshua and Caleb (those who remained faithful to God's will) survived to enter Canaan.

1. Think back to a difficult choice you had to make in the past where you put your faith in God to see you through to the decision. What decision did you make? What was the result? How satisfied were you with the outcome?

2. Now think back to a situation where you did not trust God: maybe you did not pray for guidance and instead tried to control the outcome on your own. Or perhaps you refused to listen to God's message. Compare that outcome with your responses to question #1.

3. What fork in the road are you currently facing (or may face in the future)?

4. How can you put your trust in God and remain faithful to His plan for your life as you make that decision?

4. If you are not facing any forks in the road, what can you do today to prepare for any difficult choices you may face in the future?

STUDY GUIDE

Chapter Five

How do I Handle My Mistakes?

Everyone makes mistakes: it's an unavoidable part of life. But how well you handle your mistakes will determine how easily you can move on in a positive direction. Sometimes people refuse to forgive themselves for their mistakes, and this inability to move forward keeps them stuck in a vicious cycle of resentment, doubt, and shame. Other times, people refuse to forgive someone who wronged them, and neither person is able to move beyond the pain from the past.

The sooner we come to view adversity and mistakes as learning experiences, the sooner we can tap into the power of God's glory – and live the life that He has intended for us. While it is important to feel remorse, confess to God, and make amends for our actions, it is equally important to seek forgiveness – and then actually forgive ourselves for mistakes! Likewise, we must forgive others who may have caused us harm, making way for them to move on (and to allow ourselves to move past the negative experience as well).

Please turn to the story of the prodigal (lost) son (found in Luke 14: 11-32) to learn more about the power of true forgiveness and reconciliation. After reading this moving story, please feel free to answer the questions below.

Questions for Adult Groups

Two sons. One son always remained faithful to his father, obeying his commands and living a reputable life. The other son took his father's money and squandered it through his wild lifestyle.

Thrown into poverty, the son realized the error of his ways and cried out to God for forgiveness. Soon after, the boy returned home, and his father welcomed him back with open arms.

Although the father had every reason to let his son suffer the consequences of his poor decisions, he decided to forgive his son. The brother who had remained loyal did not understand his father's actions at first; in fact, he argued that it "wasn't fair" that the father took the son back with no questions asked. However, with compassion and empathy, the father made it clear that returning home and learning a lesson were more important. He did not make his son "pay" for his actions forever. Instead, he simply forgave him and allowed him to return home and reconcile with the family.

1. When in your life were you like the wayward son, either by straying from God, hurting others, or making poor choices?

2. At what point did you realize the error of your ways?

How did you make amends (to yourself, God, others, etc.) or ask for forgiveness? (Note: If you never made amends or asked for forgiveness, is there any action you could take today to begin the healing process?)

3. Is there anyone in your life who has hurt you in the past? If so, have you forgiven him/her? If not, consider offering forgiveness to that person...even if you don't think he or she "deserves" it. Remember, holding onto a grudge is hurting you, too.

4. Consider a time you faced adversity. How was it a learning experience for you? If you never thought of it in these terms before, take some time now to acknowledge any lessons you can learn (for instance, what to do differently next time, what *not* to do, etc.).

5. Discuss with the group any current adversity you are facing. Ask them to brainstorm ways that you may end up learning valuable lessons from your experience, no matter how challenging your current circumstances may be.

Questions for Teens

Two sons. One son always followed the rules and listened to his dad. The other son, meanwhile, wasted his father's money on parties and selfish pursuits. After losing it all, the wayward son realized his mistake and cried out to God for forgiveness.

Soon after, the boy found his way back home, and his father forgave him for his wild ways. Although the father had every reason to let his son suffer the consequences of his poor decisions, he decided to forgive his son. The brother who had remained loyal did not understand his father's actions at first; in fact, he argued that it "wasn't fair" that the father took the son back with no questions asked. However, with compassion and empathy, the father made it clear that returning home and learning a lesson were more important. He did not make his son "pay" for his actions forever. Instead, he simply forgave him and allowed him to return home and reconcile with the family.

1. Have you ever been like the lost son? Maybe you've strayed away from God, hurt other people, or made decisions that you knew were wrong. If you feel comfortable sharing, describe those experiences with your group.

2. When did you realize you had made a mistake? How did you try to make up for it or ask for forgiveness (from God, others, etc.)? (Note: If you never made amends or asked for forgiveness, is there any action you could take today to begin the healing process?)

3. Is there anyone in your life who has hurt you in the past? If so, have you forgiven that person? If not, consider offering forgiveness...even if you don't think he or she "deserves" it. Holding onto a grudge is hurting you, too.

4. Consider a time you faced adversity. How was it a learning experience for you? If you never thought of it in these terms before, take some time now to acknowledge any lessons you can learn (like what to do differently next time, what *not* to do, etc.).

5. Discuss with the group any difficulties you are currently facing, whether it's at home, school, or in one of your relationships/friendships. Ask the group to help you brainstorm ways that you may end up learning valuable lessons from your experience, no matter how challenging your current circumstances may be.

STUDY GUIDE

Chapter Six

Can I Really Overcome These Challenges?

Although everyone experiences low points in their lives, those challenges, heartbreaks, disappointments and traumas do not need to last forever. There are ways to overcome even the worst circumstances... and determination is a key ingredient that will allow you to recover, overcome, and succeed.

You may wish to refer to the brief parable of perseverance (Luke 18:1-6) as you continue to work with your study group to answer the questions below.

Questions for Adult Groups

This short Bible story illustrates the importance of perseverance. In this case, a widow refuses to give up after asking the town's judge to help her seek justice against an adversary. At first, the judge tries to ignore her, but eventually her persistence and prayers pay off – and the judge brings justice to the widow.

1. Describe a time when you faced difficulties and could not muster the determination to make it through. What happened? How did you feel? If you could turn back time, is there anything you might have done differently? What have you learned through the experience that may help you in the future?

2. Now think back to a time when your determination paid off. How did it feel? How did you remain determined during that period in your life? How did you stay focused?

3. Sometimes it's easy to make excuses or blame others during times of struggle. What excuses have you made in the past that have hindered your ability to remain determined?

4. What excuses are you making right now? Ask the group to provide support in moving beyond excuses and renewing your determination to persevere through any difficult circumstances.

5. The people who surround you play an important role in your life. First, make a list of the friends and family members who are closest to you. Then circle the names of those who are most supportive of you, and put a star next to the people who are positive influences in your life. Pay close attention to the names that have both a star *and* a circle, for these are the people who will challenge you to be your best – and will encourage and support you every step of the way. Discuss your findings with the group.

Questions for Teens

This short story illustrates the importance of perseverance. In this case, a widow asks a judge to help her bring an adversary to justice. At first, the judge ignores the woman, but she refuses to give up. Eventually, her persistence and prayers pay off – and the judge brings justice to the widow.

1. Describe a difficult time in your life where you were not able to remain determined to work through the situation positively. What happened? How did you feel? If you could turn back the clock, is there anything you might have done differently? What have you learned through this experience that may help you in the future?

2. Now think back to a time when your determination paid off. Maybe you put in extra time studying for the test (and got the A), practiced the musical piece for hours (and nailed it during the recital), or refused to listen when everyone told you that you would never make the team (but you made it anyway!). How did it feel? How did you remain determined during that period in your life? How did you stay focused?

3. Sometimes it's easy to make excuses or blame others during times of struggle. What excuses have you made in the past that made it difficult to remain determined?

4. What excuses are you making right now? Ask the group to provide support in moving beyond excuses and

renewing your determination to persevere through any difficult circumstances.

5. The people who surround you play an important role in your life. Make a list of friends and family members who are closest to you. Then circle the names of those who are most supportive of you and put a star next to the people who are positive influences in your life. If you listed a name without a star or circle, ask yourself why that may be the case. Meanwhile, pay close attention to the names that have a star *and* a circle, for these are the people who will challenge you to be your best – and will encourage and support you every step of the way. Discuss your findings with the group.

STUDY GUIDE

Chapter Seven
It's Never Too Late . . . Start Now!

As you follow God's will for your life and forge your own path, you will find that instead of following the crowd, you may be *leading* the crowd! This makes it even more imperative that you don't lose sight of your purpose so you remain committed to your goals. But what are your goals? What actions do you need to take to keep in a right relationship with God as you strive to be your personal best?

Please turn to the following verses to learn more about what God has to say about goals: Luke 14: 28-31; Proverbs 13:16; Proverbs 16:3; and Philippians 4:13.

Questions for Adult Groups

These verses highlight the importance of goal setting and keeping your eye focused on God when considering those goals. The following questions will challenge you to think about your life purpose in a more concrete way so that you can start today and begin taking steps right now that will help you achieve your goals.

1. Think about your life's purpose (see your responses from Chapter 3). To fulfill that purpose, what steps or milestones will you need to achieve along the way? List them now and share your list with the group.

2. Choose one of the milestones, as this will be your first goal. Write your goal on a piece of paper. When wording your goal, consider writing it in "S.M.A.R.T." format. That means you want the goal to be specific (S), something you can measure (M), attainable (A), realistic (R), and time-bound (T).

   For example, maybe you're a financial planner, and one of your goals is to help people build a portfolio that aligns with their personal values and morals. In this case, one of your goals may be to create a comprehensive list of solid investments that you can recommend to clients. Your S.M.A.R.T. goal for this milestone might be: "I will take twenty minutes each day to research and identify at least ten solid investment options for one client by the end of this month.

   Here is another example: If your purpose in life is to write a book, but you are not sure what you want to write about, perhaps your first S.M.A.R.T. goal would be: "I will spend 10 minutes each day brainstorming and journaling my thoughts over the next two weeks.

Once you have written your goal, please share it with the group.

3. Next, create two more S.M.A.R.T. goals and share those goals with the group.

4. Commit to a date and time when you will begin working toward your first goal, and get started! The next time your group meets, check in with each other to monitor your progress.

Questions for Teens

These verses highlight the importance of goal setting and staying focused on God when thinking about your goals. The following questions will challenge you to think about your life purpose in a more concrete way so that you can start today and begin achieving your goals right now!

1. Think about your life's purpose (refer to your answers in Chapter 3). To fulfill that purpose, what steps or milestones will you need to achieve along the way? List them now and share your list with the group.

2. Choose one of the milestones, as this will be your first goal. Write your goal on a piece of paper.

When wording your goal, consider writing it in "S.M.A.R.T." format. That means you want the goal to be specific (S), something you can measure (M), attainable (A), realistic (R), and time-bound (T).

For example, maybe you want to be a veterinarian, and you're currently a high school student. In this case, one of your goals may be to begin getting more experience working with animals. Your S.M.A.R.T. goal for this milestone might be: "I will call five local veterinarians in my area this week and ask if there are any volunteer opportunities at their practice."

Here is another example: If your purpose in life is to act, and you know it's important to work with an acting coach, perhaps your first S.M.A.R.T. goal would be: "I will save half of my money from my part-time job so, by the end of this month, I will be able to afford a coaching session."

Once you have written your goal, please share it with the group.

3. Next, create two more S.M.A.R.T. goals and share those goals with the group.

4. Commit to a date and time when you will begin working toward your first goal, and get started! The next time your group meets, check in with each other to monitor your progress.

STUDY GUIDE

Chapter Eight

Your Heart Holds the Key
to Your Purpose

To have a heart after God's heart, we must spend time alone with Him. However, some people can't stand to be alone. They fill every moment with noise from the radio or TV. They feel a need to be around people constantly. Unfortunately, it is not possible to grow in the things of God unless you make time to spend alone with Him.

I suggest you read Chapter 16 in 1 Samuel to learn more about the importance of developing a strong relationship with God – which can only happen when you devote silent time in prayer and communion with Him.

As you work through the discussion questions in this final chapter, I will challenge you to begin some new habits that will help you put "heart over matter" in your daily walk with God.

Note: Due to the length of each question/discussion topic in this chapter, your group may wish to break up Chapter 8 over the course of several weeks, depending on the amount of time you have for each session.

Questions for Adult Groups

In this Scripture, David was out in the field with his father's sheep when a messenger, out of breath, came running up and said, "The prophet Samuel is with your family, and he wants you to come!" So David went, and to everyone's bewilderment, Samuel anointed David as king. I doubt if anyone except Samuel understood at that time the full significance of that act. But they knew it meant something.

Samuel went back to Ramah, but where did David, the newly anointed king, go? Back to his sheep! And what did he do out in the fields with those sheep? Fortunately, he didn't have an iPhone or television – or else we wouldn't have the Psalms! Instead of distracting himself, David used that time alone to develop his relationship with God.

1. For most of my twenties, I was alone. I had a lot of alone time in cities where I knew almost no one, and it would have been easy to fall into sin – and nobody would have known. If you're married with children at home, you probably will have to fight to make time to spend alone with the Lord. And if you're single, you'll have to fight to use the time you have alone for spiritual growth rather than for yielding to temptation. What distractions and temptations in your life make it

difficult for you to find time to spend alone with God? Discuss your thoughts with your group.

2. Read your Bible! One easy way to start making time for God is to learn to read. Personally, I haven't always been a reader. God used a friend to challenge me to start reading books to strengthen my spiritual life, and now I can't find enough time to read. Remember, reading is a learned skill. Even if you aren't good at it now, you can learn. Perhaps you should begin by taking a reading course at the library or by reading a book on how to read better. Once you learn to read, it opens up treasures from the greatest Christians of all time. Nothing has helped my spiritual life more than reading.

Read your Bible over and over again, cover to cover. The godly George Muller read his Bible over 200 times. He read through his Hebrew Old Testament seven times! As you read, don't do it to check it off your list of things to do. Read prayerfully, asking God to reveal Himself and to show you your own heart, with a view to obedience.

Make a commitment to begin reading your Bible today. What time of day will you carve out to read? How long can you devote to reading? How many days each week will you commit to? Share with the group your plans for making time to read.

3. Learn to pray. Use alone time to commune with God. Read

and pray the Psalms, which reflect David's communion with God. Study the Lord's Prayer and Paul's prayers as models. Take some silent time to pray – just time between you and God. Then reconvene with your group and share your insights and discoveries.

4. Learn to worship. Our public worship on Sundays should be an overflow of our private worship. Learn to adore God and marvel at His love in your time alone with Him. You can worship through song as well! Sometimes we forget that the Psalms were not just poems; they were set to music. God seeks those who worship Him. After attending a worship service, meet with your group to discuss how the experience allows you to keep God closer to your heart.

5. Finally, serve God. As you reflect on your strengths, talents, life purpose, and goals, continually ask yourself how these relate to what God wants for your life. As you form a close relationship with God, you will sense when your motives, actions, and words are in alignment with God. Think about a time when you felt that you were in a "zone": tapped into God's will for your life, and acting on His will. What were you doing? How did it feel? Discuss with your group.

6. What was the most important message that you have taken away from reading this book? Share your insights with your group, and be sure to continue to fellowship together as you continue on your journey.

Questions for Teens

In this Scripture, David was out in the field with his father's sheep when a messenger, out of breath, came running up and said, "The prophet Samuel is with your family, and he wants you to come!" So David went, and to everyone's bewilderment, Samuel poured oil on David's head to show he would be king. I doubt if anyone except Samuel understood the full significance of that act. But they knew it meant something.

Samuel went back to Ramah, but where did David, the newly anointed king, go? Back to his sheep! And what did he do? Fortunately, he didn't have an iPhone or television – or else we wouldn't have the Psalms! Instead of distracting himself, David used that time alone to develop his relationship with God.

1. For most of my young adult life, I was alone. I spent a lot of alone time in places where I knew almost no one, and it would have been easy for me to fall into sin without anyone even knowing it! It's also easy to get busy and distracted. Between school, friends, hobbies, and jobs, there is so much going on in life that it's difficult to find time for spiritual growth. What distractions and temptations in your life make it difficult for you to find time to spend alone with God? Discuss your thoughts with your group.

2. Read your Bible! One easy way to start making time for God is to learn to read. Personally, I haven't always been a reader. God used a friend to challenge me to

start reading books to strengthen my spiritual life, and now I can't find enough time to read. Remember, reading is a learned skill. Even if you aren't good at it now, you can learn. Work with a trusted teacher at school or tutor to improve your skills, or ask a friend to help. Once you learn to read, it opens up treasures from the greatest Christians of all time. Nothing has helped my spiritual life more than reading.

Read your Bible over and over again, cover to cover. The godly George Muller read his Bible over 200 times. He read through his Hebrew Old Testament seven times! As you read, don't do it to check it off your list of things to do. Read prayerfully, asking God to reveal Himself and to show you your own heart, with a view to obedience.

Make a commitment to begin reading your Bible today. What time of day will you carve out to read? How long can you devote to reading? How many days each week will you commit to? Share with the group your plans for making time to read.

3. Learn to pray. Use alone time to commune with God. Read and pray the Psalms, which reflect David's communion with God. Study the Lord's Prayer and Paul's prayers as models. Take some silent time to pray – just time between you and God. Then reconvene with

your group and share your insights and discoveries.

4. Learn to worship. Our public worship on Sundays should be an overflow of our private worship. Learn to adore God and marvel at His love in your time alone with Him. Singing is a form of worship, too! Sometimes we forget that the Psalms were not just poems; they were set to music. God seeks those who worship Him. After attending your next worship service, meet with your group to discuss how the experience allows you to keep God closer to your heart.

5. Finally, serve God. As you reflect on your strengths, talents, life purpose, and goals, continually ask yourself how these relate to what God wants for your life. As you form a closer relationship with God, you will sense when your motives, actions, and words are in alignment with God. Think about a time when you felt that you were in the "zone": tapped into God's will for your life, and acting on His will. What were you doing? How did it feel? Discuss this with your group.

6. What was the most important message that you have taken away from reading this book? Share your insights with your group, and be sure to continue to fellowship together as you continue on your journey.